Learning to Teach English

Peter Watkins

Published by
DELTA PUBLISHING
39 Alexandra Road
Addlestone
Surrey KT15 2PQ
England

E-mail: info@deltapublishing.co.uk
www.deltapublishing.co.uk

First published 2005

ISBN 1 900783 74 6

Photocopiable pages

Edited by Xanthe Sturt Taylor
Designed by Christine Cox
Illustrations by Phillip Burrows
Project managed by Chris Hartley
Printed by Halstan & Co, Amersham

Author's acknowledgements

I would like to thank Nick Boisseau and Chris Hartley for their guidance and unstinting support for this project. I would like to thank Xanthe Sturt Taylor for her editorial expertise and suggestions. I would also like to thank Linda Taylor, Jenny Pugsley, Roger Hunt and Rebecca Platt for their helpful comments on various drafts of the manuscript.

Dedication

For Sarah and Charlie

Contents

Introduction

English language teaching (ELT)

For various historical and economic reasons there is a huge demand for English language training in many parts of the world. The needs and circumstances of those wanting instruction vary enormously, but the majority of them want contact with a teacher, whether it's through a structured course, or through individualised private lessons, and therefore the demand for teachers is very high. It should be remembered that with such diverse needs and differing contexts in which teaching takes place, there is no one 'right' way to teach. However, the techniques and methods described in this book give teachers a starting point from which they can modify their practice to suit the needs of individuals and particular groups. It is certainly true that simply being an expert user of English, whether as a native or non-native speaker, does not guarantee that someone will make a good teacher. The skills of teaching still have to be learned.

The term 'English language teaching' suggests that 'English' can be neatly defined as a single entity. However, it is probably more accurate to talk of 'Englishes', taking into account the different varieties of English spoken. The English used in the USA, for example, is slightly different to that used in Britain and differences can be seen even between regions of Britain. In addition there is the English that is used between non-native speakers for whom English is a common language but not a first language. It is important to remember that no one particular variety of English is intrinsically 'better' than any other and English language teachers can come from any linguistic background. This book is written in standard British English and the examples are taken from a British English teaching context. However, the methodology could be applied to teaching any variety of English, or indeed any language.

Who this book is for

This book is designed to help people who want to become teachers of English to adults. Many people embark on what they hope will be a rewarding career by enrolling on an initial training course such as The Cambridge CELTA course or a Trinity College *London* Certificate in TESOL course. This book will prove a useful preparation for such courses, as well as a useful reference tool throughout the course.

Any initial training package will usually present a lot of new material and ideas in a short space of time. This can be very daunting and when thrown into a first job a new teacher can often struggle to recall all the information from the course. This book will help by being a permanent record of ideas that can be referred back to for as long as necessary.

Some people are not sure if a career in ELT would be right for them. This book will help to convey the nature of what teaching involves on a day to day basis and can therefore help to inform their decision on whether to pursue ELT as a career.

Some people may know that a long term career in teaching is not for them but may be planning to travel and would like to supplement their money with some informal teaching as the opportunities present themselves. This book is an efficient way of picking up basic teaching techniques without spending a lot of time and money following a course.

If you are starting out, or thinking of starting out, on a career in ELT this book will be useful to you. It is written to be easily understood by those with no previous experience of teaching. Many of the chapters also include ideas for activities that can be used directly in lessons, and in this way the book provides support both during initial training courses and when teachers take up their first jobs.

How to use this book

When someone is reading material on a subject of which they have little experience, it is easy to fall into reading in a very passive manner. You read the words but they are not fully processed, and as such the information is difficult to recall even a short time later.

This book aims to make the reader more active and so enhance the chances of material being both fully understood and remembered. There are many questions and activities to think about and complete as you go through the book. If you have no experience of being a teacher, it may be that you will not have thought about these topics before. However, we all have notions of good and bad teaching practice (sometimes based on our school experiences) and the tasks will help you to review what you already instinctively feel about teaching. The answers to the questions and activities are contained in commentaries following each chapter, and sometimes these commentaries also supply additional information.

For those completely new to ELT it may be best to work through each chapter in chronological order. However, those who have had some training or experience can use the book as a reference to read about areas of particular interest.

It is important to remember that this book is an introduction. There are many complex issues in teaching, but topics are dealt with as simply as possible here. There are often alternative techniques and strategies that can be used in situations but sometimes, for the sake of simplicity, only a limited range is given here. As teachers gain experience, so they often find ways of adapting techniques to benefit their particular classes, but this book will help to give a foundation on which to base, and evaluate, alternative techniques. It is important to remember that what is described in these pages is **a** way to teach, not **the** way to teach.

CHAPTER 1

Language, learning and teaching

This chapter will look briefly at the nature of language, the nature of language learning, and the relationship between learning and teaching. These are complex areas and there is much that researchers are still uncertain about, but some understanding of what is already known, and what researchers currently think about language and language learning, is an essential first step before looking at classroom teaching techniques.

The nature of language

Language is a vast subject and it is beyond the scope of this book to do anything more than to introduce very briefly some of the most important points.

Units of language

Words – letters and sounds

When written down words are made up of letters, and when spoken they are made up of sounds. In some languages the pronunciation of a word may be fairly easy to predict from the sequence of letters, but in English, for example, there is a relatively weak relationship between the spelling of a word and its pronunciation. For instance, it is difficult to predict the final sound in 'thorough' from the 'ough' letter combination, as the same combination of letters represents a very different sound in 'enough'.

Words and morphemes

Look at the words in bold in the following sentences:

1 I have a **cat**.
2 She likes **cats**.
3 I **love** her.
4 We **loved** each other very much

We can see that in sentences 2 and 4, the words 'cats' and 'loved' are made up of two parts. The 's' in cats indicates that the word is plural – we are not talking about just one cat, but all cats. The *-ed* ending of 'loved' means that as well as the core meaning encompassed by 'love', we also know that the past is referred to. So the word 'loved' consists of two meaningful parts. These parts are called **morphemes**. Morphemes may have a grammatical function (just as the *-ed* ending indicates the past), or they may add a lexical, or 'dictionary' type meaning. For example, *un* in 'unhappy' has a lexical meaning – it has the meaning of 'not'. 'Happy' clearly signifies a completely different message to 'unhappy' whereas 'happy' and 'happiness' share the same basic meaning, although one is an adjective and one is a noun. Morphemes may be 'bound' or 'free'. Free morphemes can stand alone (as words) but 'bound' morphemes must be attached to another morpheme. So, 'unhappy' has two morphemes, 'happy' is a free morpheme and 'un' is a bound morpheme. How many morphemes are there in these words?

1 teacher

2 postgraduate

3 unselfish

When you are ready, check your answer on page 12.

Sentences

Individual words can be joined together to form chains. These chains are usually called sentences and they traditionally have a subject and a verb. However, in spoken language the chains may not always correspond to what we traditionally expect a sentence to be like. For example:

Ken: Can you give me a hand?

Sue: Just a minute.

'Just a minute' has no verb, but may still be referred to as a sentence. There are 'rules' which only allow certain combinations of words. 'Minute a just' is a very unlikely combination and 'me give you a hand can' makes the original meaning unintelligible. The way in which words combine into sentences is called **syntax**.

Texts

Sentences rarely exist in isolation. Typically they combine with other sentences. In recent years there has been growing interest in the way in which language operates at this 'above sentence' level. Such study gives insights into such things as how sentences are combined and also the ways in which speakers and writers refer backwards and forwards to other parts of the text.

So, part of a teacher's job is to help learners to learn new words, and to help them to combine these words effectively.

Form, function, context and meaning

Look at the following exchange:

James: Do you mind if I open the window?

Sonia: Well, actually I'm really cold.

This exchange can be analysed in several ways. The **form** of the language can be analysed. That is to say, the underlying grammar patterns. Sonia says 'I'm really cold', which is a subject pronoun (*I*), followed by the verb *to be* (*am*), followed by a modifying adverb (*really*), followed by an adjective (*cold*).

The **function** of the language could also be analysed. 'Do you mind if I open the window?' is asking for permission to do something. There are many other ways that James could have asked for permission. 'Would you mind…?', 'Can I…?' and so on would have performed the same function, but the actual choice of words will depend on the **context** of the request – such things as who is being asked, the relationship of the speakers and what permission is being requested for.

The form and function of the language may guide us to a likely range of meanings, but the precise meaning can only be seen in the context in which the language is used. Here, Sonia says 'I'm really cold' and this effectively denies permission. It acts as a polite way of saying 'don't open the window'. However, if she said 'Well, I'm really cold' in the context of speaking to her doctor about symptoms of an illness, the message would be interpreted differently. So we can say that the meaning of a piece of language is context dependent.

Spoken and written language

Look at the following pieces of language. Do you think they were originally written or spoken?

1 It is with pleasure that we offer you the post of research assistant.

2 Look, I know you mean well, but the thing is we… this isn't what I want.

3 Having interviewed over fifty people who live in the region, it seems that we would have to conclude that there is a lack of support for the project.

4 Everyone you ask around here will tell you, they'll tell you, we don't want it.

When you are ready, check your answers on page 12.

We will examine the differences between spoken and written language in more detail in Chapter 10. At this point it is sufficient to say that there are marked differences between the two modes of communication and that people tend to speak more than they write. This means that learners often need to develop oral skills more than writing skills. On the other hand, the written form of language is often accorded a particular prestige and some learners may need to develop these skills, particularly if they need English for business or academic purposes. It should be noted that it cannot be assumed that a learner who is good at speaking will necessarily be good at writing, or vice versa. There is often a significant variation in a learner's abilities in different areas.

The nature of language learning

Most language teachers have, at some point in their careers, probably felt frustrated that some of their learners have failed to learn something which the teacher thinks s/he explained very clearly, or else seems so easy that they expect all learners to remember it immediately. In the teaching of English, for example, the adding of an 's' when the third person singular form of a verb is used in the present – the difference between *I walk*, *you walk*, but ***she** walks* – seems straightforward. And yet teachers often find that despite constant correction and reminders, learners continue to say 'she walk' for some considerable time.

A popular metaphor to explain this is to say that learners are not 'empty vessels' ready to be filled with the teacher's knowledge. However clear the teacher's explanations, there is often a delay between something being presented by the teacher and becoming fully assimilated into the learner's existing knowledge, and being available for spontaneous use by the learner when s/he wants to speak. This is not to say that all teaching is a waste of time. It may be that the teaching of some items speeds up the process by which they become assimilated. Some people argue that heightened awareness of a language feature (through overt teaching) may make the learning process more effective in the long run.

Learners are not empty vessels because there is no one to one relationship between what is poured in by the teacher and what is retained by the learner. Learners may pick up bits of language which the teacher does not set out to teach, and they may not always remember bits that the teacher does prioritise. A more accurate metaphor may be to compare language development to a plant. It will grow and develop naturally as long as it is in the right conditions. Part of the teacher's job is to ensure that as far as possible those conditions are provided, and to help learners to learn as efficiently as possible. There may be a relationship between learning and teaching but it certainly isn't neat and tidy.

Another feature of learning is that it seems to be more effective the more the learners are involved in the process. A teacher can tell learners about a language and its systems. That is to say, that teachers can try to transfer their knowledge to the learners. However, research suggests that the more that learners are involved in working out patterns for themselves, the better those patterns will be learned. So an alternative approach is for teachers to provide examples, ask appropriate questions and try to guide learners to discover things for themselves. We will look at how teachers can promote this depth of processing when we examine specific teaching techniques.

The nature of language teaching

In recent years there has been a shift to seeing language teaching as being most effective when it is subordinated to learning. In other words, the teacher's job is to help learners to learn effectively, or to facilitate learning. For example, and as discussed above, a teacher can make a choice between 'telling' learners what the teacher knows, or setting up ways of helping learners see patterns for themselves. Another way in which learning takes precedence over teaching is in the choices of what is taught and how it is taught, because these decisions should be made with the learners' needs in mind.

The best teachers have a range of techniques available to them, although of course, no teacher can possibly be aware of all the potential alternative methods available. From the range that the teacher has s/he makes a decision on those that are best suited to a particular context, based on such questions as:

Who are the learners? What are their needs? What are their expectations? What material and resources are available?

The list of potential factors that could influence the choice of approach is huge.

This can be summed up by the following diagram:

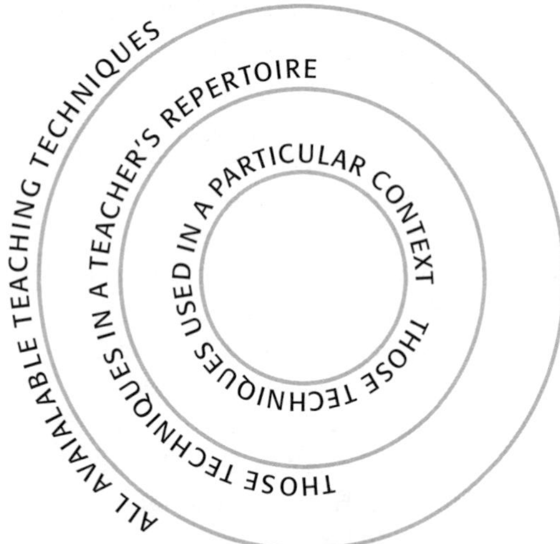

For new teachers the middle circle is naturally relatively small, and the choice of which techniques to adopt may be limited. Part of developing as a teacher is expanding the middle circle so that more choices are available. With growing experience, so it becomes easier to make appropriate choices for a particular learning/teaching context.

Approaches to learning and teaching

Any book on language teaching methodology should avoid giving the impression that there is only one way to teach a language. The fact is that many people have learned languages extremely successfully over many years while being exposed to a variety of methodologies. Teachers should be wary of following dogmas blindly. Instead they can develop their skills by being prepared to reflect on their teaching and learn from their experiences. It should be remembered that different teaching contexts give rise to different problems, which inevitably call for different solutions.

However, as a starting point for their reflection and development, teachers can learn from what others have done before them and what is often considered to constitute best practice today.

Look at the following brief descriptions of teaching techniques. Have you experienced any of them? If you were learning a language, would you like to experience them? In what ways do you think they would, or would not, be useful?

1 The teacher presents grammar rules by explaining them using the learners' mother tongue. Learners practise these rules by translating sentences both from and into the target language. Learners are expected to learn lists of words in the target language with their mother tongue equivalents. Speaking practice is not considered very important.

2 The teacher provides a spoken model of a short piece of language. Learners repeat it several times and try to memorise it. The teacher corrects any mistakes. Taped material may be used and may include gaps where learners supply the missing words.

3 The teacher does not organise the course around a list of traditional grammar points but instead sets up a series of communicative situations, similar to those that learners may find themselves in in real life. So learners will learn how to order a coffee, how to ask for directions, ways of making suggestions, and so on.

4 At first learners just listen and do not speak until they feel ready. When they do, the teacher responds to meaning, rather than the grammatical form, and the teacher does not draw attention to any grammar points.

When you are ready, read the commentary on page 12.

Communicative approaches

What has developed as the prevailing methodology used in teaching English in many parts of the world today can be loosely termed the 'communicative approach'. However, it is in itself something of an umbrella term, covering a variety of teaching strategies which are bound together by placing an emphasis on developing communicative competence. In other words, 'knowing' a language involves being able to use that language effectively in real life situations. Many people make a broad distinction between what *Thornbury calls a 'shallow end' approach and a 'deep end approach'. In the deep end, or strong form, communication is dominant and language systems (grammar, vocabulary and so on) are focused on in so far as they affect a particular piece of communication. So, learners may talk about television programmes, and the language taught will spring from the discussion and what learners appear to need in order to take part effectively.

In the shallow end, or weak form, a piece of language may be preselected and taught, but the teacher ensures that there will be opportunities to practise that piece of language in communicative contexts as the lesson progresses. So, the teacher may decide that the lesson will focus on the present perfect simple and will then choose practice activities that allow this pattern to be reinforced throughout the lesson. It is this weaker form which dominates the vast majority of EFL text books, and it also informs the majority of teacher training courses, at least at pre-service level. New teachers should be able to select an appropriate piece of new language to teach their learners, and provide a variety of practice activities to reinforce learning. The approach tends to highlight the need for the explicit teaching of vocabulary, grammar and functional language (ways of making suggestions, agreeing, disagreeing and so on) as well as the need to give direct practice in speaking, listening, reading and writing.

In both the strong and weak form of the approach there is a great emphasis on learners working in pairs and groups. Part of the rationale for this is to maximise the amount of speaking practice that can be provided for learners in a single lesson.

These approaches, and particularly the skills needed by a teacher using the dominant weak form of the communicative approach, will be the main focus of the following chapters.

Summary

- Language is made up of morphemes (meaningful bits of words), words, sentences and texts.
- Language can be analysed into form, function and meaning (which is dependent on context).
- Language learning may be helped by learners working things out for themselves.
- Learning and the learner should be prioritised over teaching and the teacher.
- There are various language teaching approaches and methodologies that can be adopted.
- The communicative approach prioritises an ability to communicate over a knowledge of 'rules'.

*Thornbury, S (1999) *How to Teach Grammar* (Longman)

CHAPTER

1 Commentary

The nature of language

Words and morphemes

1 two – *teach* is the root and the *-er* suffix (ending) indicates that this is the person who does teaching.

2 two – *graduate* and the prefix *post*, with the lexical meaning of 'after'.

3 three – *un* (meaning 'not'), *self*, and the suffix *-ish* which indicates this is an adjective.

Spoken and written language

1 Written
2 Spoken
3 Written
4 Spoken

Approaches to learning and teaching

1 This is a very brief description of the 'grammar-translation' method. Up until the 1940s it remained the dominant method of teaching, and is still used, often in modified forms, in some places today. It relies on the teacher having a fairly expert command of both the mother tongue of the students and of the target language. The learners must all share the same mother tongue. The emphasis is on learning grammar rules and it is assumed that these will lead to an ability to communicate. However, this is not necessarily the case because there is a difference in knowing about a language (its rules and so on), and actually being able to use the language. The lack of emphasis on language as a means of communication is a major drawback. Also, most research suggests that bilingual word lists are not the most efficient way of learning vocabulary, partly because most words do not have a direct equivalent in other languages. Learners need to know how words relate to other words in the target language at least as much as knowing how they relate to those in their first language.

2 This is a very brief description of the audiolingual approach. It became popular through the 1940s and remained so until the early 70s. The benefits of repetition are still intuitively recognised by many teachers today, and this element of the approach continues in many classrooms. However, the theoretical principles underpinning the approach, particularly that language is about habit formation, were attacked by linguist Noam Chomsky. He argued that the human mind had an innate ability to process language, allowing people to comprehend and produce utterances they had never heard before – thus destroying the idea that habit formation is responsible for language development.

3 This is a very brief description of a functional approach associated with, among others, David Wilkins. It should be noted that the term 'functional' is used in different ways by different people but here refers to the defining of the communicative functions that learners are likely to want to engage in (making requests, agreeing, disagreeing, ordering a coffee and so on). The approach gained popularity through the 1970s and remains an element of many courses.

4 This is a very brief description of the natural approach associated with Stephen Krashen. It attempts to recreate as closely as possible the context in which infants learn their first language. Despite the claims that have been made for the successes of this approach, most researchers, and certainly most students, believe that some overt teaching of language 'rules' is useful.

CHAPTER 2

Roles of teachers and learners

Different roles of the teacher

'What does a teacher do?' The obvious and simple response is 'a teacher teaches', but what do we mean by this? What does teaching involve? The answer to this is bound up with the idea of how people learn. As we saw in the previous chapter, there is not a one to one relationship between teaching and learning. Although teachers can tell learners about language – tell them what words mean, give grammar rules and so on – this does not seem to lead automatically to learners being able to use the language that they are 'given'. Learners may learn things from the teacher, or from each other, or from watching a film, or hearing a song, reading something, or perhaps by reflecting on things that they have been 'taught' in previous lessons. Sometimes learners will seem to make quite rapid progress, and at other times progress will be slow. Sometimes learners will need a significant amount of time (days, weeks, or months) before something they have been 'taught' really makes sense to them and they feel able to use it. Although teachers try to make teaching an orderly and organised business, learning remains apparently chaotic. Teachers of languages have to accept this and set about helping people to learn at their own pace and in their own ways.

We will look at some of the roles teachers adopt to try to facilitate learning. Although teaching strategies may vary according to the subject matter, the group being taught and so on, we can see certain patterns emerging in all teaching, and quite clear patterns when we look at language teaching.

Try to picture a lesson that you have experienced, if possible as a language learner (or teacher) but if that is not possible, think of any lesson. Think in as much detail as possible. Write down as many actions that the teacher performed as you can. For example, the teacher gave instructions to the class. Are there any other actions you associate with teaching?

When you are ready, compare your list to the one below, which has been based on a language lesson. (Don't worry about the numbered left hand column for the moment.)

1	The teacher gave instructions to the class.
2	The teacher encouraged students to speak and participate.
3	The teacher listened to what students said.
4	The teacher mimed a series of actions.
5	The teacher spoke in the target language and found material for the class to use.

6	When students spoke their own language the teacher told them to use the target language.
7	The teacher answered the students' questions.
8 *language guide*	The teacher helped the students to work out grammar patterns for themselves.
9	The teacher checked that all the students were present and ticked a register.
10	The teacher watched the students work in pairs or groups.
11	At the end of the course, the teacher set a test.
12	After each lesson the teacher thought about what was successful and what was less successful and tried to decide why.

Of course, your list will probably be different to this one, and there are more things that could be added to the one above. However, it gives an idea of how teachers spend their working lives. Many of the actions described above will happen on a daily basis and, although some may be more central than others to the general skill of teaching, they all play a part.

Look at the different roles that a teacher has in the box below, and match these 'labels' to the descriptions in the list above. The first one has been done as an example.

language guide	expert resource	performer
reflector	observer	assessor
prompter	provider of input	listener
administrator	organiser	controller

When you are ready, check your answers with those on page 17.

The value of these roles

The importance to teaching of some of the roles introduced in the previous section may seem immediately more obvious than others. In this section we will look in a little more detail at what each role involves and why it is important.

Most institutions will have their own administrative procedures that teachers will be expected to follow. These may include preparing reports on students, keeping records of what has been taught, and preparing a plan of a sequence of lessons to be taught. Teachers may well be expected to assess their students by administering a test or tests at some point either during, or at the end of, a course. However, unlike the other roles, these two functions are removed from day to day contact with students. It is these day to day activities that we will now look at more closely.

Look at the situations described below. For each one say which of the teaching roles needs to be focused on for the lessons to become more successful. For each role try to think about precisely what it involves and why it is important.

Example:

1 The teacher has arranged the class into eight pairs and each pair is talking to each other. One pair finishes the exercise very quickly and then the students say very little to each other. **Observer**

2 The students complain that they don't like the material being used in the lessons because it isn't relevant to them.

3 The teacher's lessons are well planned and the material seems interesting but the students often complain that they feel bored during them.

4 A student asks a grammar question but the teacher is unable to answer it.

5 The teacher asks the students to work in groups to discuss a topic. A few students do but most ignore the teacher and chat to each other in their own language.

6 The teacher usually explains grammar by standing at the front of the class and telling the students about the new language. Students often seem to forget these rules and seldom apply them.

7 The teacher feels that s/he is no longer improving as a teacher.

8 The teacher asks the students what they think about crime. Nobody answers.

9 The students like activities in which they talk in pairs and groups but sometimes feel frustrated because they know they make mistakes but the teacher rarely corrects them. The learners ask for more correction but the teacher answers that they didn't make any mistakes.

10 The teacher gives instructions on how to do the following activity, but when the class starts doing the activity they all do different things.

When you are ready, read the commentary on page 17.

Different roles of learners

The learners' task in the teaching and learning equation is to construct the system of the target language. They have to find out and remember how words are joined together and what they mean, how grammar patterns fit together, as well as how phonological features such as stress and intonation are used. The system the learner constructs can only emerge gradually – parts may come from direct, conscious learning of new bits of language, and other parts may be subconsciously picked up from exposure to the target language.

The ways in which learners undertake this daunting task will vary according to the learning styles each individual prefers, their previous learning experience, their own perceived needs and so on. However, just as we were able to analyse roles of the teacher, so we can analyse certain roles that learners will fulfil. Again as with the roles of the teacher, the list is not exhaustive and there is some overlap between them.

Look at the roles below. How might learners benefit from being effective in each?

Participant
Discoverer
Questioner
Recorder of information

When you are ready, compare your notes with those on page 18.

Helping learners to fulfil those roles

The responsibility of fulfilling these roles is shared between the teacher and student. In this section we will look at what teachers can do to help students fulfil their roles successfully.

To help learners to fulfil the role of **participant** the teacher could

- invite students to respond (see role of prompter)
- provide group and pair work (see role of provider of input)
- value contributions made by praising and responding appropriately (see role of listener)
- respect when students do/do not want to speak and reflect on why this may be the case

We will now look at the roles of questioner, discoverer, and recorder of information. In each case, answer the questions.

When you are ready, read the commentary on page 19.

Discoverer

1 Which role of the teacher does this relate most to?

2 Which approach, described below, do you prefer, A or B?

A The teacher says…
'The past simple is formed by changing the infinitive of the verb so that it ends with *–ed*. 'Work' becomes 'worked', 'play' becomes 'played' and 'behave' becomes 'behaved'.'

B The teacher says…
'Look at these examples: *work – worked, play – played, behave – behaved*. What pattern can you see?'

3 Above all, give students the chance to discover rules and patterns for themselves by resisting the temptation to supply all the information too quickly. True or false?

Questioner

To help the students the teacher could teach a phrase such as 'How do you pronounce *sign*?'

4 What other similar questions could the teacher teach?

5 Above all, create an atmosphere in which students feel able to ask questions. True or false?

Recorder of information

6 What common classroom aid would a teacher need to be able to use to help learners with this?

7 How can you help students to make **complete** records?

8 How can you check that students are keeping records?

Summary

- Teachers have various roles. All are important and need to be understood by the teacher.
- Analysing these roles helps reflection on professional performance and therefore professional development.
- Learners perform various roles.
- By consciously helping learners to fulfil these roles, teachers can help them to learn more efficiently.

CHAPTER

2 Commentary

Different roles of the teacher

1 organiser
2 prompter
3 listener
4 performer
5 provider of input
6 controller
7 expert resource
8 language guide
9 administrator
10 observer
11 assessor
12 reflector

The value of these roles

1 *Observer*

By observing the class carefully you can ensure that everybody is doing what you want them to do. You can also watch for any sign of students who seem to particularly enjoy or dislike working with each other. You can also see what kind of activities the students enjoy. This role is clearly linked to the role of **listener**. Careful observation will also show when learners have finished – the teacher may want to provide extra extension material and practice for learners who finish particularly quickly. This therefore also links **observer** to the role of **provider of input**.

2 *Provider of input*

Part of a teacher's job is to ensure that learners work with suitable material. It needs to be varied, fit in with the interests of the students and be at an appropriate level. Quite often the teacher will be able to select material from a course book. Even by speaking naturally in English during lessons, teachers provide valuable input for students. For more on the teacher's use of language, see Chapter 3.

3 *Performer*

To be an effective teacher you do not have to be an entertainer. The focus of the lesson should be more on the students than the teacher. However, there are elements of performance in some aspects of teaching. At certain times you need to be able to address relatively large groups, and to do so confidently. You need to use your voice and also gestures effectively. You also need to sense when students are becoming bored and need a change of focus. Without these very basic performance skills, lessons may be unsuccessful, however well they have been prepared.

4 *Expert resource*

When asked to define a good teacher (of any subject), learners typically respond that they should 'know their subject'. This is no different in language teaching. As well as knowing their subject, teachers must also be able to explain it in a clear way that students can understand. Typically non-native speaker teachers can fulfil this role very well because they have had to learn the language by going through the same processes as their learners. Native speakers, on the other hand, while instinctively knowing if something is right or wrong, can find it difficult to analyse a language which they use so instinctively. This role should be compared to, and not confused with, that of **language guide**, where the focus is on helping learners to work out rules for themselves.

5 *Controller*

Problems with discipline in adult classrooms are relatively rare but even so the teacher must be prepared to act occasionally to ensure that a suitable learning environment is maintained. Teachers should aim to be polite but firm, and ensure that students follow basic rules. Probably the most fundamental rule is that they must respect other people in the class (including the teacher), and this means, amongst other things, listening to what people are saying. For more on issues concerned with discipline, see Chapter 3.

6 *Language guide*

As expert resource we discussed the need for the teacher to know their subject. Language guide deals more with how knowledge is conveyed to the students. Simply explaining language relies on a model of knowledge transfer: I know it – you don't – I'll tell you. There are problems with this model. Learners are not very involved in the process and this can lead to a fairly shallow understanding and lack of retention. Of course, there are times in the language classroom when students ask questions, perhaps not directly related to the lesson, when it is appropriate to use this model. However, a more powerful model may be when the teacher, as a language guide, helps the students to construct their own system of knowledge, which can be deeper and more meaningful to the learner. Typically this is achieved by asking questions and prompting students to discover patterns and rules for themselves, so that they are thoroughly involved in the learning process. For more on this, see Chapter 4 and following chapters.

7 *Reflector*

All teachers, regardless of their experience, need to reflect on what they do. We need to think of what went well in a lesson and what didn't, so that we can try to improve. A list of roles, such as this one, can help teachers analyse their strengths and weaknesses and so guide their future development. Having experienced colleagues watch your lessons, reading books and articles about teaching, and taking advantage of any workshops available can also help you to reflect on your own practice and continue to develop as a teacher. For more on professional development, see Chapter 18.

8 *Prompter*

Part of a teacher's job is to encourage students to speak. Sometimes students need very little prompting but sometimes it can be harder. Amongst other reasons, reluctance to speak can stem from a lack of confidence or from cultural expectations regarding how lessons should be conducted. Sometimes simply nominating a particular student by name may help, because some students are reluctant to volunteer themselves but are happy to speak when invited. In this example the lack of response may indicate that the learners are unsure of what is required. 'Crime' is quite an abstract topic to address and it is difficult to know from the question the type of response expected. The teacher could help the situation by giving a more concrete example. Rather than saying 'What do you think about crime?', a description of a specific example ('This person has broken into 10 houses but never hurt anyone. Should he go to prison?') may be easier for students to relate and respond to. In other activities the role of prompter may be slightly different. At times a student may be speaking but then not be able to think of how to continue. The teacher could step in and prompt by sensitively asking an appropriate question so that the flow of communication can continue.

9 *Listener*

By listening teachers can detect the individual strengths and weaknesses of a student and respond to them. Teachers can give appropriate feedback. New teachers can sometimes find it difficult to respond to what students say effectively. This is often because they are very concerned with what they will be doing next and their own performance. When students are talking in pairs or groups it can be useful to take notes, so that you remember what you heard after the activity.

10 *Organiser*

A teacher needs to plan and carry out the 'mechanics' of the lesson. How many people will work in a group? Which students will work effectively together? What instructions do students need? How can you make instructions clear – will an example and/or a demonstration help? How long should an activity take? Where will students sit? What will you do about late arrivals to the class? The list of questions is almost endless but for a successful lesson these types of issue need to be considered, just as the language input is planned.

Different roles of learners

Participant

By participating fully in the lesson students gain practice. They can 'test out' how they think the language works in a non-threatening environment and may benefit from feedback from the teacher on their efforts. Practice in using language and exposure to it seem to be important elements in the learning process. However, teachers should be aware that some learners may feel uncomfortable about joining in in certain situations, and some people may prefer to remain relatively quiet and observe others. Many people may learn very effectively in this way, and so learners need the opportunity to participate, but not necessarily be forced to.

Discoverer

This is strongly linked to the teacher's role of language guide. By taking the opportunities to work out patterns and rules for themselves, learners can benefit in the ways described in that section.

Questioner

This is linked to the above role. By asking questions learners can take responsibility for their own learning to some extent. They can set the agenda of what gets taught, rather than simply being the passive recipient of what the teacher presents. They can also tap into and benefit from the teacher's expertise.

Recorder of information

When we have to remember something important most of us write it down. This means that we can refer back to the information. Learners need to record new words and phrases, new bits of grammar and so on, to help them remember what they learn. They can also make these records outside the classroom when they study independently.

Helping learners to fulfil these roles

1 Language guide.

2 Assuming that this is the main focus of the lesson rather than a response to an unrelated question, then B is usually better.

3 True

4 What does ____ mean?
How do you spell *umbrella*?
When do we use the *present simple*? (or some other verb form).
How do you say….? etc.

5 True

6 Whiteboard – so that students can copy things down.

7 The teacher could give models of good records and give students advice on what to record.

8 Occasionally check note books, or simply ask students.

CHAPTER

3 Managing a class

In the previous chapter we looked at the various roles that a teacher is called upon to fulfil. In this chapter we are going to look at two of these roles, 'organiser' and 'controller' in some detail. Being able to organise a class is every bit as important as understanding the nature of language or how languages may be learned. Without basic classroom management skills any lesson can quickly degenerate into chaos. One of the most important skills a teacher needs to develop is how to grade their own language so that it is appropriate to the class they are teaching. Having considered this, we will then go on to look at one of the biggest concerns for most new teachers, the issue of controlling the class. We will conclude the chapter by briefly looking at how common technological aids can be exploited effectively in the classroom.

Grading language

There are many good reasons for conducting as much of a lesson as possible in English. On a practical level, native English speaker teachers may not know the language of their learners well enough to make use of that language. Also, many classes may be made up of learners from a range of countries, which makes it impossible to use any language other than English.

At a more theoretical level, it should also be remembered that one of the main prerequisites to developing language skills is exposure to the language, and therefore using English as much as possible is essential. In addition, using too much of the learners' first language can send a negative message, as it implies that the teacher does not trust the learners to understand English. There may be occasions on which a teacher considers it useful to use the learners' first language, for example to reassure learners, or explain methodology at lower levels. However, even in these circumstances it is probably best to limit the amount of language other than English used.

However, using English is problematic. Particularly at low levels of language competence, learners can find it difficult to understand and can soon become confused and demotivated. What can teachers do about this? Four of the following pieces of advice are intended to be good, but one piece is poor advice. Which one?

1 Select the language used carefully. Try to avoid complex vocabulary and grammar choices. Compare:
'OK, if you wouldn't mind stopping there for a moment, because there's another activity I want you to have a go at before we do some reading and listening practice.'
and
'Stop there, please. I want you to do another activity.'

2 Pause for slightly longer than normal after each thing said.

3 Do not speak too quickly.

4 Miss out grammar words, such as articles and prepositions. For example: 'You go now office – they help you.'

5 Wherever possible, support what is said with other things that will help understanding (gestures, pictures and so on).

When you are ready, read the commentary on page 25.

Adjusting your language for the level of the learners you are teaching can be very difficult, but is a very important teaching skill. It is important that the models you give learners remain reasonably natural because learners will pick these up. The language which it is appropriate to use with a low level class will be significantly different to the language used with a higher class, although it should remain natural. It is not necessary that learners understand every word you say – many researchers would argue that the language used should include new features because it will provide learners with the raw data from which they can learn – but learners must be able to understand your overall message.

Classroom management

As part of a training course a group of trainee teachers were asked to teach a lesson, and then write an entry in a journal summing up what happened, and their thoughts and feelings on the lesson.

Read the extracts from what the trainee teachers wrote and consider the questions that follow each extract.

Claire: *The lesson would have been OK I think, but the students have a real problem understanding what I say to them. Today one student asked me to speak more slowly.*

1 As well as speaking more slowly, what else can Claire do to make herself easier to understand?

Mark: *I tried to use some pair work* (where one learner speaks to another) *so that the learners would get more practice, but with everyone talking the lesson was quite noisy and I was worried in case another teacher complained.*

2 Should language classrooms always be quiet?

Becky: *I stood up at the beginning of the lesson but most of the time I sat down because I think it is important to be comfortable.*

3 When you were at school did your teachers generally stand up or sit down?

4 Can you think of some reasons why teachers may choose to stand or sit?

Bill: *It was awful today. We were doing something on past forms but a student asked me something about gerunds and I didn't know the answer, so I just had to say 'sorry I don't know' – it was so embarrassing.*

5 Do you think teachers are right to admit their ignorance when they don't know?

Karen: *Last week I made a huge effort to learn the names of everyone in the class and today I got them right every time – so I was quite pleased.*

6 Do you think that Karen was right to put such store by knowing the names of her students?

7 In what situations can knowing the names of the learners help?

Jack: *I knew I wanted the learners to work in groups so that there would be a lot of interaction, but when I said 'get into groups' nobody did anything, and most of the students just worked on their own.*

8 Do you think it was a good idea to use group work?

9 Who should decide on the groupings, the teacher or the students?

10 Can all activities be done as group work?

Ellis: *I wanted the learners to read a text really quickly just to get the idea of what it was about, but they all read really slowly and worried a lot about new words, which wasn't the idea at all.*

11 How could Ellis have avoided this problem?

Ken: *In the past my lessons have been OK except for when I write on the board. My writing isn't very neat at the best of times, and when I start writing on the board nobody can read anything. I also find everything gets mixed up and I run out of space.*

12 Should you write in upper or lower case, or both?

13 Should you print everything or use joined-up writing?

14 How can you stop the board getting so confused?

Susan: *I wanted to nominate a student to speak but didn't know her name, so I pointed to her instead and she answered, but after the lesson another trainee told me that he thought it was quite rude to point in that way.*

15 Who do you agree with, Susan or her colleague?

Tom: *I asked a question to the whole class and everyone started speaking at once! I didn't know what to do.*

16 Was Tom right to worry about this?

17 How could Tom have ensured that only one learner spoke?

Kath: *I was doing an activity with all the students talking to each other, mingling round the room, and it was going really well. There was quite a lot of noise and when I tried to stop the activity, they couldn't hear me and just carried on talking. I couldn't stop them!*

18 How would you have stopped the activity?

Steve: *I try not to use too many gestures because I think adult learners must find them a bit patronising. I use a few more when I teach kids.*

19 Do you think using gestures is a good idea?

Laura: *I planned this really nice activity and I'm sure it would have been good, but the students didn't understand what I wanted them to do and it all went wrong.*

20 How can instructions be kept simple and easy to understand?

When you are ready, read the commentary on page 25.

Complete the following summary of the points in the above section by putting one word from the box below into each gap.

instructions	board	expectations	language
strategies	gestures	distinguish	

Summary of classroom management

Good teachers …

- grade their own ____________ so that it is appropriate for their learners
- respect their learners and their learners' ____________
- ____________ between useful and non-useful noise
- use the ____________ effectively
- can give ____________ and manage learning activities effectively (set up pair work etc.)
- use ____________ effectively and without causing offence to learners
- have ____________ for dealing with situations when they don't know something

When you are ready, check your answer on page 26.

Discipline

Discipline is not usually a problem with most groups of adult learners. The majority of learners have chosen to attend the class and understand the sort of behaviour that is and is not generally considered acceptable. However, very occasionally problems do arise, and teachers need to know how to respond to them. Such problems can be more frequent when teaching children. A group of experienced teachers were asked for their views on discipline. Read them and say if you agree or disagree.

		Agree	Disagree
1 Kevin:	*It's just a job – never get upset by anything a student says to you.*		
2 Olga:	*Keeping order is about authority and you either have it or you don't.*		
3 Frank:	*Whatever else you do – make sure that learners don't use their own language.*		
4 Julie:	*I always try to embarrass a student who is doing something wrong and this way they are less likely to do it again.*		
5 Stewart:	*Most problems can be ignored and eventually they will go away.*		
6 Roger:	*The most important thing for a new teacher is to ask why there is a problem and then tackle the root cause.*		
7 Sandra:	*Keep a professional distance from learners – be friendly but don't try to be friends.*		
8 Monica:	*Move around the room a lot during a lesson and try to keep in touch with everything that is going on.*		
9 Sharon:	*Most problems occur when students get bored or have nothing to do – so don't let the lesson slow down too much.*		
10 Gabriel:	*I sometimes negotiate some rules with the class and write them on a noticeboard. Everyone (including me) has to sign this and it is like a contract.*		
11 Carla:	*The most important thing to do is find out the policy on discipline of the school you are working in.*		

When you are ready, read the commentary on page 27.

Using technological aids

A further aspect of classroom management is the efficient use of some of the technological aids which are frequently found in many modern classrooms. We will look at each in turn, but it is important in all cases that teachers check that the equipment is working before the lesson and that they know how to operate it.

CDs and audio tapes

Audio tapes or CDs are usually supplied as part of a course book package and are obviously very useful in providing listening practice for learners. Teachers need to ensure that tapes are in the correct place before the lesson and, where possible, use the counter on the tape recorder so that the tape can be rewound to the correct original position after use because learners will usually need to listen more than once.

As well as using audio tapes for listening practice, students often find it very motivating to be recorded when speaking. This can be very useful because learners can speak freely and then listen to the tape and correct any mistakes that they hear or the teacher points out.

Videos and DVDs

Videos and DVDs can provide a useful variety of input. They are often used as a source of material for listening practice, where they are particularly useful because of the visual information, such as body language, which forms part of communication. However, they can also be used as a prompt for practising other skills. Some videos are produced specifically for English language teaching, and these have the advantage of grading language and tasks so that they are appropriate for even low level classes. They also usually come with worksheets, making them easy for teachers to exploit.

Teachers may also have the opportunity to record programmes from the television to use with classes, although it is important to respect copyright laws. Material recorded from the television can be chosen for its particular relevance to a group of learners and can therefore be very motivating. However, a disadvantage is that the teacher will usually have to spend considerable time devising appropriate tasks to help the learners follow the programme and benefit from it.
As with audio tapes, video can be used to record learners, for example, as they perform a role play.

Overhead projectors

Overhead projectors allow teachers to prepare before the lesson what they want to show students. The transparencies can be prepared using coloured pens or can be photocopied on to. One of the advantages of using overhead projectors is that teachers can take time to prepare diagrams, example sentences, grammar exercises and so on without having to write them on the board under pressure during the lesson. By covering parts of the transparency with paper, the teacher can control when things are revealed. Another useful activity using the overhead projector is to set up writing activities for learners, perhaps in pairs or small groups, which can be written on a transparency and then displayed immediately for the rest of the class to read.

Computers

Computers can be used for a variety of purposes in English language teaching. The internet is a good source of material for both students and teachers. There are also many software packages that can be used for learning and teaching. When these are exploited in the classroom it can be useful to group two or three learners to each computer so that they can share ideas (in English) and have a different experience to that possible when studying alone.

Summary

- Teachers need to grade their language appropriately.
- Clarity is important in all aspects of teaching, including the language used, instructions given, the grouping of learners and so on.
- Discipline is rarely a problem in adult classes.
- Where discipline is a problem, talk to the learner(s) concerned privately, not publicly.
- Where discipline is a general problem, consider involving the class in drawing up a 'contract' of acceptable behaviour.
- When using technological aids, ensure that the equipment is working and that tapes are set at the correct place.

CHAPTER

3 Commentary

Grading language

1 Good advice. The second instruction is clearer for lower level students because both the grammar pattern and the vocabulary is simpler. The last part of the first instruction is omitted in the second version. Generally it is sensible to only give instructions that the learners need immediately. Anything else can be said later, and learners are more likely to understand if they focus on a smaller amount of language.

2 Good advice. Delivering each phrase naturally but pausing for slightly longer between each phrase, is likely to boost comprehension more than just slowing down the delivery of each word.

3 Good advice, but notice that this is not the same as saying 'speak unnaturally slowly'. We all speak at a range of speeds, depending on the situation we are in, so a teacher needs to speak at the slower end of this range, but still naturally.

4 BAD advice. Learners need to be exposed to as much natural language as possible.

5 Good advice. Using such visual things will help the learners understand the meaning the teacher wants to convey.

Classroom management

1 See 'Grading language' above.

2 Classrooms cannot always be quiet. If people want to learn to speak, they will have to do some speaking. If they only speak to the teacher nobody will get enough practice, and the practice that is provided will all be of one type (quite formal, and with an unequal power relationship between the participants). Therefore teachers must provide some pair and group work, and this will generate some noise. Teachers need to distinguish between useful noise and non-useful noise. Useful noise will come from people speaking the language, students moving around or learners needing to release energy or frustration. The teacher needs to judge when the noise is serving no useful purpose and then try to reduce it. Usually most colleagues will be in a similar situation and will therefore be quite tolerant of any noise.

3 and **4** There is no simple answer to whether teachers should sit or stand as it will vary with the context of the teaching. With small groups, sitting down can be useful because you assume equal status with the group and it can help to foster an intimate atmosphere. However, with larger groups, standing up can give the teacher more authority and it leads you to move around the room more. Among other factors, the decision will be based on the group and the nature of the activity.

5 Some teachers know quite a lot about language before they ever get into a classroom. This tends to be true of non-native speaker teachers who have been through a similar learning process to those that they are teaching. Other teachers know relatively little, and it is an area on which they need to work as they pursue their professional development. In this particular case, the learner asked a question which was not directly related to the aim of the lesson and therefore it may have been best not to go into much detail, even if the teacher had felt confident to do so. The priority for new teachers is to understand the language point they are teaching in some depth, so that they can answer questions related to the lesson. There is nothing wrong with admitting ignorance sometimes and saying 'I'll find out for you', but this strategy cannot be overused, and must be followed through by remembering to tell the learners what you find out. Even if the teacher does know the answer, if the question is not relevant to a particular lesson, a phrase such as 'Can we come back to that later?' may be useful.

6 and **7** Names are important in teaching, not least because the use of someone's name can help to make them feel valued and respected as an individual. This is very important in a language classroom. Knowing the names of your learners can help when setting up pair work (telling people who should work with whom), getting the attention of someone who is not looking at you, and in many other situations. It is usually worth devoting some time in the first lesson with a group to getting to know everyone's name. It is also useful for the learners to know each other's names because they will need to address each other during lessons.

8, **9** and **10** For the reasons stated previously, group work is often a good idea, although in some contexts (such as when very large classes are being taught) the teacher may feel that it is impossible. Group work may also run contrary to some learners' expectations. Some learners expect a fairly teacher dominated lesson, and in these situations it is a good idea to introduce pair or group work in small doses and be prepared to explain the reasons for using it. In most situations it is usually best if the teacher organises it and tells the students clearly who is working with whom. Learners can sometimes feel awkward about arranging themselves in groups, and the teacher may have reasons for combining certain students (mixing nationality groups, language level and so on). Clearly some activities must be done individually. Learners cannot read or listen together for example, although they can later discuss what they have read/listened to.

11 There are several ways that Ellis could have avoided this problem. The activity itself will often dictate how it is done, because questions which ask for a certain type of information often demand certain types of reading skill. For example, the teacher could set a task which only necessitates gaining an overall impression of content. Such tasks may include the learners choosing the best two line summary from a choice of two or three or asking them to choose the most likely source of the text – a newspaper, a novel, a magazine and so on. Another simple solution would be for the teacher to have used a time limit – telling the learners how long they had to complete the task. She could also have explicitly told the learners not to worry about new words, while reassuring them that they would get the opportunity to read in more detail later.

12, **13**, and **14** New teachers often worry about writing on the board but most people find it quite easy, and even those who don't can improve very quickly, with just a little practice. As a general rule it is a good idea to write on the board using upper and lower case, just as you would on paper. Use upper case where it is appropriate, and lower case everywhere else. The main justification for this is that what the teacher writes on the board is a model for learners to copy, and therefore the model should be accurate and natural, as far as possible. It is probably a good idea to print (rather than use joined up writing) for most things that you write on the board because it tends to be easier to read. It could be argued that this is **not** a natural model (see above) but the importance of this will depend on the extent to which learners need to read handwritten texts, as most texts they need to read are likely to be printed. Some teachers find it useful to consciously divide up areas of the board for different purposes (an area for new vocabulary, a separate area for error correction, and so on) and even divide the space up physically by drawing lines on the board. This is a useful strategy for teachers who find that their board quickly becomes cluttered and confused otherwise.

15 Generally it is a good idea to try to avoid pointing because in some cultures it can appear very aggressive. However, sometimes teachers do need to indicate in this kind of way. Typically a gesture with the hand quite low (around waist height) with the palm of the hand facing up seems less aggressive. Teachers need to be sensitive to which gestures and language are likely to offend their learners. Offence can sometimes be caused accidentally by an insensitivity to, or lack of awareness of, cultural differences.

16 and **17** Tom was right to worry about this. Although at times you may want lots of interaction (in group work, for example) you can't have everyone speaking to the same person! The easiest way to prevent this from happening is to nominate the student you want to speak by using their name, or perhaps through eye contact or a gesture such as the one described above.

18 This is not an easy situation for most teachers to deal with. Some new teachers feel uncomfortable in exerting their authority but there are one or two occasions when you need to and this is one of them. One way is to project your voice in such a way that it remains authoritative and can be heard. A teacher can also give a loud clap, or make some other signal. The class will soon get used to the signals adopted by the teacher.

19 Gestures are a natural part of face-to-face communication, although the degree to which they are used may vary from culture to culture. Typically they are extremely useful in the ELT classroom because they can support the message that you are trying to convey – and communicating successfully with learners is a vital part of language teaching. The lower the language level of the group being taught, the more important gestures become.

20 As Laura found, even the best activities can go wrong if the instructions are not carefully planned. Instructions need to be delivered in simple language. They sometimes need to be backed up and reinforced by the teacher giving demonstrations with a member of the class, or working through an example with the class before the learners work independently. If they are particularly complex it can be worth checking that the learners have understood what they should do before they start an activity. If the learners do misunderstand and start to do the wrong thing, the teacher should be prepared to stop the activity and try giving the instructions again.

Summary

Good teachers ...

- grade their own language so that it is appropriate for their learners
- respect their learners and their learners' expectations
- distinguish between useful and non-useful noise

- use the board effectively
- can give instructions and manage learning activities effectively (set up pair work etc.)
- use gestures effectively and without causing offence to learners
- have strategies for dealing with situations when they don't know something

Discipline

1 This is generally good advice and if you do feel upset, it is often best to try not to allow it to affect the way you deal with a situation. The way in which learners will regard a teacher may vary from culture to culture. In some cases learners hold teachers in high esteem and would not readily criticise. In other cultures there is a smaller power differential between teachers and learners. If teachers teach learners who are used to expressing negative views more bluntly than the teacher is used to, then offence can be caused, and it is useful for teachers to remember the cultural perspective. However, not getting upset does not mean not listening to or thinking about something. If a student complains about an aspect of a lesson, it is worth reflecting on what has been said and trying to work out if there is something behind it which could improve your teaching.

2 'Authority' is difficult to define. Some people certainly do seem to exude confidence and seem assured in front of a class, but to some extent this can be learned and may spring from careful preparation and planning.

3 One of the most common problems that teachers face is that learners who share the same mother tongue (or another common language) will use it. Occasionally this can be quite helpful because learners may use their own language to support each other. However, often it is not used in such a constructive way, and as a general rule as much should be done in English as possible. If you are teaching a mixed nationality group the problem is diminished and those learners that do share a language can often be split up. In cases where the teacher feels there is a problem, s/he may find it useful to have 'rules' of when the mother tongue can be spoken. For example, after twenty minutes of using English the learners get a two minute break to say what they want in their own language before the lesson re-starts.

4 Generally this is not a good idea. Learners, like everyone else, need to retain 'face' and a degree of self respect. Embarrassing people removes this and will only create a situation in which learners do not want to come to the lesson. Adults must be treated as adults at all times – and that means with respect. Children too need to be respected and left with a positive view of their learning experience so that at the very least they will want to carry on learning. Once disaffected, learners are more likely to cause the teacher problems.

5 This may occasionally be the case, but more often problems grow into bigger problems and it is usually best to deal with them early on. Often it is enough to talk to a student privately, perhaps at the end of the lesson, and go through the kinds of behaviour that you find acceptable and not acceptable, as well as asking about any particular views or feelings that the student may want to express. In other words, the teacher gives the learner the chance to explain why s/he is being disruptive.

6 This is a good piece of advice, and links to number 9 below. There may be something that the teacher can do that will help the situation.

7 Again this seems good advice.

8 Again this seems good advice. The teacher needs to be aware of all the learners in the room and what they are doing, and this is easier if the teacher moves around at some points in the lesson.

9 Boredom can certainly be a cause of problems. It may be that the teacher needs to provide a little extra work for those students who finish an activity first, or perhaps in a class where there are problems, activities should be brought to an end slightly earlier than usual so that learners are kept focused. Again, careful monitoring of activities (see 8 above) can help the teacher to make these decisions.

10 This is a very useful strategy and necessitates a discussion of rules and allows learners to have some input into how they feel a class should be run. Once written down, learners often respect the class rules more than before. A golden rule should be that everyone must respect others in the class, and this includes listening to what they have to say.

11 Again, this is a very sensible piece of advice. In the very rare cases where discipline is a serious problem it is important for the teacher to know where they can turn for help, when they have done all that they can reasonably do to solve the problem themselves.

CHAPTER 4

Teaching vocabulary, grammar and pronunciation

Systems and skills lessons

Some lessons focus on grammar, some on vocabulary and others on helping learners with pronunciation. These types of lessons focus on the patterns and systems that underpin the language, and most learners feel a need to learn at least parts of these systems. An awareness of how the language works may help students to perform more effectively when they have to speak, listen, read or write. Lessons which focus on these underlying systems try to help learners to see the 'rules' of a language.

Other lessons focus directly on speaking, listening, reading and writing (the so called 'four skills'). Such lessons are usually referred to as **skills** lessons and could be seen as practice for the sort of 'real world' activities learners are likely to want to perform. Learners need to speak to others, listen to information, write notes and so on. **Systems** lessons, on the other hand, aim to improve performance in these skills by developing an awareness of the patterns of language that underpin them. It is easy to assume that systems can be built up block by block, with a teacher explaining a new piece of language and the learners then being able to use it. However, both experience and research evidence suggests that teaching rarely impacts on learning quite so neatly. Rather than systems being built in discrete blocks, it seems that learners' awareness of language grows and new information is gradually assimilated into the developing systems. This means that teachers need to be prepared to return to certain points later in the course, give lots of practice, and be prepared for learning to be, at times, a slow process.

We will look later at skills lessons, but this chapter will look at some of the things that vocabulary, grammar and pronunciation lessons have in common.

Presenting language

There are many ways in which new language can be introduced to a class. Look at the following examples and answer the questions that follow.
When you are ready, read the commentary on page 32.

Method 1

The teacher writes a sentence on the board – 'Laura has lived in New Zealand for two years.' The teacher says: 'Look at the underlined part. This is the present perfect. It means that Laura is still in New Zealand. This situation is unfinished. It's formed with *have* or *has* and the past participle.'

1 The teacher's explanation covers two things. What are they?

2 What is the learners' role in this case?

Method 2

The teacher writes a sentence on the board – *Laura has lived in New Zealand for two years.* The teacher says: 'Look at the underlined part. Do you know what this verb form is called? Do you think she is still in New Zealand?'

3 What is the learners' role in this case?

Method 3

The teacher uses a short text.

Laura finished university and moved to New Zealand. She has lived there for two years. She really likes it and has no plans to come back to England.

The teacher then asks: 'Do you know what this verb form is called? Do you think she is still in New Zealand?'

4 In what way is this different to method 2, above?

Method 4

The class is discussing the merits of space travel. The teacher participates in the discussion and says 'In fifteen years I think it will have become quite common for people to travel in space'. A learner asks why she used 'will have' and the teacher quickly explains the verb form before moving the class back to the original discussion.

5 Did the teacher plan to present this piece of grammar?

6 Can you think of any advantages to teaching new language in this way?

7 What demands does it make on teachers?

Method 5

The teacher gives the class some examples of how regular past forms are pronounced.

/t/		/d/		/ɪd/	
worked	talked	loved	moved	needed	shouted
walked	guessed	called	emailed	wanted	pleaded
liked	washed	listened	lived	painted	rented

She asks the class to try to work out the 'rule' for when the /ɪd/ sound is used.

8 What is the teacher's role in this case?

9 What is the learners' role in this case?

There is no right or wrong way to teach. However, as a general principle, it seems likely that learning will be more effective the more the learners are involved. This would point to methods 2, 3, 4 and 5 above being particularly beneficial. We have also noted the need for language to be used in context, which is an advantage of Methods 3 and 4. 4 could easily be adapted to involve learners more, by asking them if they can explain the usage from an example or two on the board. However, how a teacher teaches a piece of language may depend on, amongst other things, the learners, their expectations, and the aim of the lesson.

Practising language

However clearly and accurately teachers describe a piece of language, it is often the case that learners will not be able to use it effectively. One thing that learners need is the opportunity to experiment with language – to try it out – and the classroom is an ideal place for this because it provides a non-threatening environment. These opportunities to experiment can be achieved through providing practice activities.

Look at the practice activities described below and answer the questions that follow.

When you are ready, read the commentary on page 32.

(It should be noted that there are many, many ways of practising language, and these are just a few examples.)

Activity 1 – the teacher has taught ten words connected with transport. She then gives the learners ten sentences and each one has a gap. The learners have to put one of the new words into each gap. For example:

> *The police stopped him because he was driving too fast. He was breaking the ____________ by more than 40 kph. (answer: speed limit)*

1 Do the learners write or speak?

2 Do the learners produce the new language themselves, or have to recognise and understand the new language when it is used?

Activity 2 – the teacher has taught some words connected with work and employment (salary, wages, trade etc.). He then gives the class a series of short reading texts, and from a list the learners have to decide which jobs are being described. For example:

Gary: I quite like my job. The money is OK, particularly if I do a lot of overtime. I left school at 16 and I needed a lot of training, because you need to learn a trade properly before you can start working on your own.

Is Gary a waiter, a teacher or an electrician? (*electrician*)

3 Do the learners produce the new language themselves, or have to recognise and understand the new language when it is used?

Activity 3 – the teacher has taught the present perfect with the meaning of 'at some point in the past'. (*Have you ever worked in a foreign country?*) The learners have to write questions for other members of the class. They then read them out and the person addressed answers the question. For example:

Maria: Olga, have you ever been to Paris?
Olga: Yes, I have. I went there two years ago. It's very beautiful.

4 Does this practise writing or speaking?

5 Who decides what is written/spoken about, the teacher or the learners?

Activity 4 – the students have been learning question forms. The teacher then sets up a role play of a job interview. The learners prepare and then interview each other.

6 In what ways is this practice activity harder than the previous ones described?

Activity 5 – the teacher has been teaching the learners about word stress. She gives the learners a list of words and then reads them out. The learners have to mark the correct stress pattern on each word.

7 Do the learners produce the new language themselves, or have to recognise and understand the new language when it is used?

There are many different ways of practising language. Some practice activities will demand that the learner recognises the form and meaning of the new language. Some will focus on learners producing the correct forms and meanings. Some will focus on only the target language point and others will demand that learners can use the new language as well as drawing on language previously learned. There is no one way to practise language – learners simply need a variety of practice opportunities and many of them.

Checking and clarifying understanding

We said in Chapter 2 that teachers need to help students to work out patterns and meanings for themselves, as this is likely to lead to a deeper understanding. However, sometimes students may need an explanation from the teacher. Regardless of how the language was originally conveyed, it is important that the teacher checks that students have understood. Quite often teachers ask 'Do you understand?' but this is flawed because some students may think they have understood even though they haven't, and on other occasions may feel embarrassed about saying that they haven't. We will now briefly look at how the teacher can ask questions to check and clarify understanding.

Asking questions

Look at this example: *I've been working here for three years*. One way of checking that learners have understood is by asking questions such as:

'When did the action start?' (*Three years ago*)
'Do I still work here?' (*Yes*)
'Is the action finished?' (*No*)

Notice that these questions focus on the key concept expressed by this use of the verb form – that the situation began in the past and is continuing.

There are some guidelines to follow in the construction of such questions. They should

- be quick and easy to answer (otherwise learners may know the answer but not be able to express it)
- focus on the defining features of the target language (i.e. how the form is different to other forms)
- as far as possible avoid the use of the target language

Look at the following questions aimed to check understanding of *If Tracy had a million pounds she would travel around the world.* Which ones do you think are useful for the checking of understanding? How would you answer those questions? Which ones are not useful?

1 What would you do with a million pounds?

2 Does Tracy have a million pounds?

3 Which countries would you like to visit?

4 Is it likely that Tracy will soon get a million pounds?

5 Is Tracy going to travel around the world?

6 Does this sentence refer to a past or a present/future situation?

When you are ready, read the commentary on page 33.

Which questions would you ask to check understanding of the following grammar patterns:

1 If Anja hadn't helped Andrew in the exam he would never have passed.

2 I **might** see Amy tomorrow.

3 He gets up late at the weekend.

When you are ready, read the commentary on page 33.

This technique of asking questions to check that students have understood can also be used successfully when teaching vocabulary. Again, it is important to focus on the key features of the language item that separate it from similar items. So, learners often confuse 'briefcase' with 'suitcase', making questions such as 'Do you put your clothes in this when you go on holiday?' and 'Do you take it to the office most days?' very useful.

What questions could you ask to check the following pieces of vocabulary?

bench
lamp
armchair

When you are ready, read the commentary on page 33.

Helping learners learn

Look at the suggestions below of things that are likely to help learning. Decide which ones you think are good ideas.

When you are ready, read the commentary on page 33.

- Make sure that learners see/hear new language again and again, not just in one lesson but over a series of lessons.
- Don't teach too much new language in one go.
- Don't try to teach all the meanings of a new piece of language.
- Write new language on the board.
- Give lots of examples of the new language in context.
- Make sure that learners have the opportunity to use new language in communicative situations.

Summary

- Vocabulary, grammar and pronunciation lessons often have much in common, particularly in the areas of conveying meaning and the need for practice.
- New language needs to be contextualised, and the meaning and form to be clear.
- There are a variety of ways to present new language.
- Learners need lots of practice opportunities.
- The learners' understanding of new language also needs to be checked.

CHAPTER

4 Commentary

Presenting language

Method 1

1 Form (*have/has* + past participle) and meaning (this started two years ago and is continuing).

2 The learners are fairly passive and their role is to try to understand, and to ask questions if they don't.

Method 2

3 In this case the teacher is attempting to involve the learners and is helping them to see patterns and meaning for themselves. The learners must use their existing knowledge and try to work out what this pattern may mean.

Method 3

4 The teacher has put the language into a short text and has therefore created some context. Notice how the context helps to guide the learners to the meaning of the new language.

Method 4

5 No

6 The learners ask about the things they want to know, rather than what the teacher wants to teach. The language is presented in context and there is a clear focus on meaning because the question arises from the communication. On the other hand, because it is unplanned, it is unlikely that the teacher will be able to provide extensive practice opportunities.

7 Preparation is difficult because the teacher doesn't know what questions will be asked. Teachers have to be confident that they will answer more or less any question, or have a strategy (such as 'I'll find out and tell you next time') for coping if they don't know. Some learners may feel uncomfortable asking a lot of questions.

Method 5

8 The teacher's role is to provide enough data for the learners to be able to work out the meaning. Also, to encourage them and help where necessary, and later to confirm that what has been 'discovered' is accurate.

9 The learners have to make guesses about the rules governing the language and then see if the evidence supplied supports their hypotheses. Such discovery techniques could, in other examples, focus on meaning as well as form.

Practising language

Activity 1

1 Write

2 Assuming the teacher rubs the new words off the board before the students do the activity, then it demands productive use of language. The teacher could make the activity easier by giving the learners a list of all the words and then asking them to select the best one.

Activity 2

3 Recognise it.

Activity 3

4 Writing (the questions), but then there is an element of speaking as the questions are read out and discussed.

5 The learners decide on the content of each question. This allows for greater learner involvement and creativity and may therefore lead to deeper processing and better learning. The teacher decides which grammar pattern should be used in the questions.

Activity 4

6 All sorts of other vocabulary and grammar will be required. This practice activity is closer to real life than the others described because more than just the new, isolated, language point is practised. Learners need to learn how to use new bits of language not just when they are told to do so, but when they have a range of choices available to them.

Activity 5

7 Recognise correct patterns. However, the teacher could ask learners to read out the words. This would make it productive, at least for some members of the class.

Checking and clarifying understanding

Asking questions

If Tracy had a million pounds she would travel around the world.

Numbers 2, 4, 5 and 6 are useful. The other two questions may be useful for discussion but do not really check that the learners have understood the piece of language.

2 Does Tracy have a million pounds? (*No*)
4 Is it likely that Tracy will soon get a million pounds? (*No*)
5 Is Tracy going to travel around the world? (*No*)
6 Does this sentence refer to a past or a present/future situation? (*Present/future*)

1 *If Anja hadn't helped Andrew in the exam he would never have passed.*

Appropriate questions may vary slightly here but the key language points are the following: this happened in the past – Anja did help Andrew – Andrew passed the exam and this was dependent on her help. Therefore questions which could be useful are:

Did Anja help Andrew? (*Yes*)
Did Andrew pass the exam? (*Yes*)
Did Andrew need Anja's help? (*Yes*)
Does this refer to the past or the present? (*Past*)

2 *I might see Amy tomorrow.*

Will I definitely see Amy? (*No*)
Is it possible I will see Amy? (*Yes*)

3 *He gets up late at the weekend.*

Is this about one particular weekend or weekends generally? (*Weekends generally*)
Did he get up late once, or does he usually get up late at weekends? (*Usually*)

Vocabulary

Possible questions are:

Bench
Is it hard or soft? (*Hard*)
Do you find it inside a house or outside? (*Outside*)
Is it for one person or more than one? (*More than one*)

Lamp
Do you find this on the ceiling? (*No*)
Can you move a lamp? (*Yes*)

Armchair
Is it soft or hard? (*Soft*)
Is it for one person? (*Yes*)
Does it have sides? (*Yes*)

Helping learners learn

All of the points are good advice.

Make sure that learners see/hear new language again and again, not just in one lesson but over a series of lessons.
This is almost certainly necessary. It seems that language learning often depends on these 'multiple exposures' to new language. Including lots of practice activities in a lesson can help learners in this way, and gives the opportunity for learners to practise using the language.

Don't teach too much new language in one go.
This would traditionally be seen as good advice, although it does depend to some extent on your view of how languages are learned. This is the approach adopted by the vast majority of materials writers and is usually popular with learners. For example, it is better to teach ten or twelve items of vocabulary and provide lots of practice, than to teach thirty items with no practice because it is unlikely that without practice they will be remembered.

Don't try to teach all the meanings of a new piece of language.
Again this is sound advice, at least at low levels. For example, if a word or grammar pattern or pronunciation pattern has more than one meaning then it is better to choose the meaning you want to convey, rather than teach them all, which could be confusing. More contrastive work may be beneficial as the learners progress.

Write new language on the board.
Good advice – it allows the learners to copy it down and refer to it later.

Give lots of examples of the new language in context.
This is very important and relates to the first point. Learners typically find examples helpful. Many researchers would argue that meeting and noticing new bits of language in context is a major influence on learning.

Make sure that learners have the opportunity to use new language in communicative situations.
Having opportunities to use new language to communicate with others seems essential to learning a language efficiently.

CHAPTER

5 Teaching vocabulary

Why you need to teach vocabulary

Learning new words is an important part of learning a new language. Even children learning their native tongue usually learn isolated words or phrases before piecing them together into more complex utterances. Learning some words and phrases in a new language allows people to start communicating at once. You could say the learners get an 'early return' on their investment of time and effort. As *Wilkins wrote in 1972 (1972:111):
The fact is that while without grammar very little can be conveyed, without vocabulary nothing can be conveyed.

Even at higher levels, successful learning of new words and phrases is often a way by which students can see that that they are making progress. So, in an approach which values the ability to communicate, vocabulary is essential, and in recent years vocabulary has become increasingly central to language teaching. Research has shown that there are strong patterns in the way in which words combine, and certain combinations are very frequent. Therefore vocabulary teaching may extend beyond the teaching of individual words to include common combinations of words, such as 'make a decision', 'by the way', or 'absolutely brilliant'.

There are a huge number of words in the language and it is impossible for the teacher to teach more than a fairly small proportion of them. Some time can therefore be usefully used in helping learners to learn effectively outside the classroom. (See Chapter 14.)

Ways of presenting vocabulary

There are many ways of teaching new words and phrases and teachers need to learn a variety of techniques, because some methods will work better with certain types of words than others, or with certain classes. A whole lesson may be spent on developing vocabulary and in this case will include suitable practice activities. On the other hand, vocabulary teaching may take place in response to a particular question or need, and in such cases may only take a few seconds, with only a brief explanation being necessary. As we mentioned above, words may be taught in isolation or in combinations.

Look at the following ways of presenting vocabulary and answer the questions that follow.

When you are ready, check your answers on page 39.

Classroom example 1

The teacher shows the class pictures of different types of transport. For each picture the teacher asks the class if they know what it is, and if not says the word, and then the class say it together before the teacher moves on to the next picture. There are six pictures in all. Afterwards, the teacher goes through the pictures again – the class say the word and the teacher writes it on the board.

1 Who gets the opportunity to say the word first?

2 Would this activity suit high level learners or low level?

3 As well as pictures, are there any other types of visual stimulus a teacher can use?

Classroom example 2

The teacher gives the class a grid, such as the one below. The learners have to tick whether they think the words along the top are used with *make* or *do*.

	a profit	*a phone call*	*business*	*your best*	*a bed*	*nothing*	*a mistake*
make							
do							

4 Can you think of any other verbs that combine with a lot of different nouns?

Classroom example 3

The teacher distributes words on cards to each student. For example, one student has *arrogant* on a card and another has *self-confident*. Another has *terrorist* and someone else has *freedom-fighter* and so on. The learners circulate, looking at each other's words and trying to find their 'partner'. When they do, they stick them on the board next to each other. There is a space on the board marked 'words we don't know'. The teacher deals with these at the end of the activity and checks the understanding of the other words.

5 What is the difference between a terrorist and a freedom-fighter? What is the difference between arrogant and self-confident?

6 Should the learners already know all the words the teacher uses in the activity, some of them, or none of them?

7 What other sort of word relationships could this activity work with?

Classroom example 4

The teacher elicits words from the learners by giving definitions. For example, 'What's the word for a thing you hold which produces light – it has a battery?'
If nobody knows the word, the teacher may give more clues, such as 'it begins with a 't' sound'. If nobody knows it the teacher tells the class. The words elicited are written on the board.

8 The teacher could have said 'What does 'torch' mean?' but what are the advantages of the approach taken in the example?

Classroom example 5

The teacher is teaching a monolingual group. A learner asks what a particular word means and the teacher translates it for her.

9 What are the limitations of using this technique?

10 What are the advantages of using this technique?

Classroom example 6

The teacher gives a list of words to the learners all related to money – *invest, earn, owe, save, waste* and so on. The teacher also supplies a list of definitions and the learners try to match the words to the definitions.

11 If the teacher were teaching concrete nouns to a lower level class, what could replace definitions?

12 What are the advantages of teaching words together that are thematically linked?

Classroom example 7

The teacher uses the word in context and the learners try to work out the meaning. For example, the teacher says, 'The dog ran into the road and the driver had to *swerve* to miss it.'

13 How could you check that learners understood the meaning of *swerve*?

Classroom example 8

The teacher uses examples to explain meaning. For example, to explain 'fruit' she says: 'Apples, oranges, plums and bananas are all types of fruit.'

> **14** Can you think of any other words, as well as fruit, that you could teach in this way?

Here is a checklist of things that a teacher may want to include when teaching new words or combinations of words:

- The form of words – how to spell them and say them
- The meaning of words – the denotation and any strong connotations
- The word class – noun, verb, adjective etc.
- Common combinations with other words (collocation)
- Any restrictions in the use of the word – for example, is it very formal/informal?
- Grammatical considerations – for example, if it is a verb, does it need an object?

Of course, not all of these things are always equally important. The teacher needs to make a decision on how much information a particular group of learners needs about any particular item.

Ways of practising vocabulary

It is essential that learners have the opportunity to practise using the new words they learn because research shows that the number of 'encounters' with a word is likely to affect how well it is learned. New words need to be practised not just in one lesson but to be 'recycled' over a series of lessons to give the best opportunities for learning.

Look at the practice activities below and answer the questions that follow.

Classroom example 1

The teacher gives the learners sentences with a word, or words, missing. The learners have to choose the best word for each gap. For example:

In my country this person is a hero because he was a great ____________. *(freedom-fighter/terrorist)*

> **1** How could this activity be adapted to make it more difficult?

Classroom example 2

The learners work in small groups to write a dialogue using different combinations of *make* and *do*. When they have finished they perform the dialogue for the class. For example:

In a meeting…

A: *We made a loss last year for the first time in our history. What can we do?*

B: *We should try to do more business abroad or think of introducing a new product.*

C: *We made a big mistake when we…*

> **2** What other language, as well as combinations with *make* and *do*, do learners need to do this activity?

Classroom example 3

To practise vocabulary relating to money, the learners work in small groups and discuss 'Is money the most important thing in life?'. After the discussion the teacher asks a member of each group to report back to the class and also corrects some of the mistakes that she heard.

> **3** What other language, as well as a knowledge of vocabulary relating to money, do learners need for this activity?

Classroom example 4

When the teacher teaches new words, she writes them on a slip of paper and puts them in a bag in the classroom. When she has a few minutes at the end of a lesson, she goes to the bag and re-elicits some of the words from the learners. Sometimes she divides the class into groups and gives each group several words from the bag and gives the groups time to make up a story incorporating the given words. After hearing the stories, there is feedback and correction.

> **4** What are some of the advantages of this technique?

Classroom example 5

The teacher divides the class into pairs. The students have similar pictures of a road/traffic scene. However, there are several differences and the learners have to describe (not show) their pictures to each other in order to find them.

5 The activity will practise the vocabulary included in the picture. What grammar pattern(s) might the vocabulary combine with?

When you are ready, read the commentary on page 40.

Some of these activities practise the new language in isolation. Others integrate the new language with existing language. Some practice activities may be spoken, others written. The essential thing is that learners get plenty of varied practice opportunities.

Choosing what vocabulary to teach

Having looked at ways of presenting and practising vocabulary, we will now go on to consider the factors which may affect a teacher's choice of which vocabulary to teach a class.

Look at the list below of some possible strategies for selecting vocabulary. Put a tick next to the ones that you think you may use.

- ☐ Teach words that are easy to teach and can be explained easily.
- ☐ Teach words that the learners may need for an upcoming activity. For example, some important new words in a reading text.
- ☐ Teach words that the learners ask about and want to know. Perhaps teach an expression such as 'What is the word for …. in English?' so that they can ask.
- ☐ Teach words that you think the learners will find useful in their day to day lives.
- ☐ Teach words that are very frequent in English.
- ☐ Teach the words that appear in the learners' course book.

When you have thought about the statements above, read the commentary on page 40.

The relationships between words

Words are defined and categorised partly by their links and relationships with other words. Learners need to know how words are similar in form and meaning, and the ways in which they are different. As learners attempt to store large quantities of words in their minds, it is to some extent these relationships that will allow them to do it successfully.

Look at the groups of words below and in each case work out how they are related.

1 political politics politician politically

2 cars bus bicycle vehicle truck

3 huge enormous massive big

4 male/female hot/cold

5 kid/child food/nosh

6 allowed/aloud been/bean

When you are ready, read the commentary on page 41.

Learners' problems and their causes

Look at the following learner errors. Each pair illustrates a different common learner problem. What is it?

1a Bill Clinton is a political.
1b Mario is a really good cooker.

2a I made this photograph when I was in Italy.
2b I'm not surprised he's ill – he's a very hard smoker.

3a (in a business letter) I'm sorry we messed up your order.
3b (to a friend) My train departs at 7.30.

4a (a Portuguese speaker) I have many parents.
4b (a Spanish speaker) My sister has two children and is now embarrassed again.

5a Let's meet ourselves at 8.30.
5b William was rude to me so I've decided to ignore.

When you are ready, check your ideas in the commentary on page 41.

Summary

- Learners need lessons which focus on vocabulary – but vocabulary may also be taught (relatively quickly) in parts of other lessons.
- Teachers may teach individual words, or combinations of words, or common phrases.
- Learners need to know how to say and write the word (or phrase) and what it means.
- Learners may also need to know about the formality of the word (or phrase), associated grammar patterns, and common combinations with other words.
- 'Multiple exposures' to new words are essential, and new words therefore need to be recycled throughout a lesson and in future lessons.

*Wilkins, D. (1972) *Linguistics in Language Teaching* London: Edward Arnold

CHAPTER

5 Commentary

Ways of presenting vocabulary

Classroom example 1

1 The students. It is generally considered good practice to try to **elicit** language from learners rather than the teacher routinely supplying it. This tends to keep interest and involvement levels high and can also be a useful diagnostic tool.

2 This technique is particularly useful for low level students because the pictures communicate meaning clearly and efficiently. In this particular example one would assume that higher level learners would already know this vocabulary.

3 There are the physical things in the classroom that can easily be used, and teachers can also bring real things into the classroom to facilitate vocabulary lessons on a particular topic. Teachers can also use mime and gesture.

Classroom example 2

4 There are many examples, such as *give, take, put, go, set, keep* and *have*, and a good dictionary will supply the nouns with which they combine. Notice that this activity is focused on the way in which words combine rather than individual words in isolation. The combination of words in this way is called **collocation**.

Classroom example 3

5 These words have roughly the same 'dictionary' meaning, or **denotation** as each other. However, the difference is in the **connotation**, or the emotional content they imply. *Self-confidence* is considered a good quality, while *arrogance* has a negative connotation. Similarly, *terrorist* has a negative connotation, while *freedom-fighter* is positive.

6 This activity works well as long as the learners know **some** of the words. If none of the words are known, then the matching is exceptionally difficult.

7 Opposites can be taught in this way (*hot/cold*) or words with similar meanings such as *hot/boiling, interesting/fascinating* and so on.

Classroom example 4

8 'What does *torch* mean?' may prove a difficult question for some learners to answer, even if they know. Particularly at lower levels, they may find it difficult to express and the lesson may become rather slow as they attempt to do so. The teacher can probably give a better and more accurate definition than most learners. Notice again that the learners get the opportunity to supply the word before the teacher tells them. Giving the first sound of a word, as in the example, often helps learners to recall a word.

Classroom example 5

9 It may encourage learners to see languages as having words which correspond precisely, but apart from in the use of concrete nouns (and not always then) this is not necessarily the case. It could be argued that learners are better served by trying to establish how a word is similar to or different from other English words, than those of the mother tongue. This method cannot be used with a multilingual class.

10 It is quick, and assuming good language skills on the part of the teacher, easy. It could be argued that learners will naturally try to translate the word in any case.

Classroom example 6

11 Learners could match pictures to words.

12 It seems likely that words are stored in the mind in related sets, or at least that this is one organisational principle. This teaching approach may help learning, therefore.

Classroom example 7

13 The teacher could ask questions (see Chapter 4) such as: 'Did the driver stop?' (*No*) 'Did they drive in a controlled way?' (*No*) 'Does 'swerve' involve the brake or the steering wheel?' (*Steering wheel*)

Classroom example 8

14 Any word that is used to represent a collection of examples of something could be taught in this way. For example, *building, vehicle* and *profession*.

Ways of practising vocabulary

Classroom example 1

1 The teacher could ask the learners to think of a word to fill the gap, without giving them the words to choose between.

Classroom example 2

2 This activity asks the learners to use the target language (*make* and *do*) and also their existing language skills. Learners will practise writing and also discuss their ideas. Depending on the context of their dialogue they will need various functional language, for example, making suggestions, agreeing and disagreeing and so on.

Classroom example 3

3 Again, as number 2 above (and unlike1) the learners need to use the new language as well as existing language skills. To take part in a discussion they will practise speaking and listening, expressing opinions, agreeing, disagreeing and so on.

Classroom example 4

4 This technique means that new words are recycled in future lessons. This is essential to successful learning. It is also useful for the teacher to have the option of a few short activities to use in spare minutes of future lessons.

Classroom example 5

5 It is likely that the learners will need to use the present progressive to describe the scene in the picture – 'Two women **are talking** to the policeman'. It could also practise 'There is…' and 'There are…'. The practice activity could be used for a wide range of vocabulary items – the teacher would simply need to change the pictures used.

Choosing what vocabulary to teach

Teach words that are easy to teach and can be explained easily.

At low levels this can be a productive strategy, particularly if all the teaching is being done in the target language. Words to do with the classroom are useful for students to know. Using lots of pictures and so on can make things easily understood, even for beginner students.

Teach words that the learners may need for an upcoming activity. For example, some important new words in a reading text.

This can be a useful exercise. Listening and reading are both very difficult if there are simply too many unknown words in the text. However, the teacher needs to be aware of whether they are teaching vocabulary for the purpose of developing students' knowledge of words, or whether they want to practise the skills of listening or reading, in which case the vocabulary can be dealt with more quickly. The teacher should not allow a lesson put aside for listening skills work, for example, to become dominated by too much vocabulary.

Teach words that the learners ask about and want to know. Perhaps teach an expression such as 'What is the word for ….in English?' so that they can ask.

This is generally good advice – there is a lot of anecdotal evidence that students can remember a word they really need or value in some way after hearing it just once. However, teachers need to guard against lessons becoming nothing but a stream of unrelated words being put on the board, requested by different students. Remember, simple exposure may not be enough for most students to learn, and there will probably be a limit to how many can be remembered. Quality is more important than quantity!

Teach words that you think the learners will find useful in their day to day lives.

Again, this is good advice because it provides a motivation to learn. The new words will actually help the students to communicate – the point of teaching! As above, it seems that learners can learn the most important things to them very quickly.

Teach words that are very frequent in English.

Frequency is a useful criterion when selecting vocabulary because students will see and hear these words most often. However, different words are frequent in different contexts and it certainly cannot be the only factor in deciding what to teach.

Teach the words that appear in the learners' course book.

The authors of most course books will have put a lot of thought into what to teach and will also ensure that new words are practised thoroughly and recycled. However, remember that no author can know your class better than you, and you may therefore find topics or vocabulary sets that would both be interesting and useful for your students. In these circumstances it is good to supplement the book you are using.

The relationships between words

1 These all come from the same root word. *Politics* and *politician* are both nouns (*politician* being the word for the person who practises politics). *Political* is an adjective and *politically* is an adverb.

2 These words are linked by a 'type of' relationship. *Cars, buses, bicycles* and *trucks* are all types of vehicle. The technical term for this is that *car* is a **hyponym** of *vehicle* (as are the other examples) and *vehicle* is a **superordinate**.

3 This group is marked by a relationship of **synonymy**. That is to say that the words all mean more or less the same thing, although you could argue that *big* is less big than the other examples. Synonymy is a relatively weak relationship in English. Although words may have similar meanings, there are often limitations on the usage of each. If you consider an example such as 'The war broke out in 1914', *break out* means something like *started* but you can't say that 'The lesson broke out at 9.00.' *Break out* is a synonym for *start* but its usage is limited.

4 These words are opposites of each other. A more technical term is that they are **antonyms**.

5 These words are again synonyms but are also marked by being either neutral in register (*food, child*) or informal (*nosh, kid*).

6 These words are **homophones** – although they are written differently they are pronounced in the same way as each other.

Learners' problems and their causes

1 The students have both had problems with selecting the right word class, and some more activities on word building (adding bits to the beginnings and endings of a root word to make new, related, words) may help. In the second example (*cooker*) the student has applied a sensible rule (add -*er* to form the person who does an action), but inappropriately in this case.

2 These errors are both to do with collocation. In English we 'take' photographs and although you can be a 'hard' drinker we use the word 'heavy' with *smoker*. Collocation is not always predictable. For example, we say 'deep trouble' but 'shallow trouble' is not acceptable.

3 'Messed up' seems too informal to be used successfully in a business letter. 'Departs' seems too formal to use with a friend. The students do not appreciate the degree of formality associated with these words.

4 The likeliest explanation for each of these is that the student is confused by a **false friend**. A false friend is when a word in the mother tongue looks like an English word and so the student guesses that it means the same, but in fact it has a different meaning in English. Usually such guessing is a useful strategy but not in these cases! In Portuguese *parentes* means 'relatives' (similar words exist in Spanish and Italian). In Spanish *embarazada* means 'pregnant'.

5 The learners do not appreciate the grammar associated with the vocabulary that they are using. *Meet* is not a reflexive verb and so we do not use 'ourselves' and *ignore* is followed by an object – *ignore* ***him***.

CHAPTER

6 Teaching grammar

What is grammar?

Grammar looks at two things. First, there is morphology – how morphemes are put together to make words (see Chapter 1). The second part of grammar is syntax – the way in which words are combined. 'I need to talk to you' is an acceptable combination in English, but 'I you talk to need' is not. So, grammar refers to the underlying patterns of the language. It looks at how units combine to make bigger units.

Grammar, however, is about more than just the form of the language. It also involves meaning. 'The boy chased the dog' and 'The dog chased the boy' are both acceptable combinations but clearly carry different meanings. 'The boy was chased by the dog' is a variation on the second example and it too has a different emphasis. Language learners therefore need to know far more than just how to form sentences. They also need to know the meaning of the forms they use **and** how to form patterns to encode the meanings they wish to convey.

Grammar descriptions designed for teaching and learning purposes are called 'pedagogic' grammars. Such grammars lack the detail of some linguistic descriptions and may make quite broad generalisations, but are often helpful in the context of learning a language. Traditionally grammar descriptions have been based on written sentences. However, modern grammar descriptions increasingly look at how units of spoken language combine and also at how units of language combine over longer texts – for example, how sentences join together and relate to each other.

The above description of grammar looks at grammar from the perspective of a particular language – so, you can look at the grammar of English, Italian or Chinese, for example. However, grammar could also be looked at from the perspective of a particular learner and how that person uses language. At the start of learning, a person's grammar is likely to be very different to models of native speaker language, (or that of expert non-native speakers) but in time it will move closer to the target. In other words, the grammar of learners emerges and, in time, becomes more sophisticated, and gradually moves towards the models that can be seen in native speaker use, having gone through many transitional stages. Part of a teacher's job is to help learners move 'their' grammar closer to that of expert users.

What are grammar 'rules'?

Grammar rules are usually described as being either prescriptive or descriptive. Prescriptive rules say how language should be used. An example of a prescriptive rule would be:

> *You must use 'fewer' with countable nouns (fewer people) and 'less' with uncountable nouns (less money). Do not use 'less' with countable nouns.*

Prescriptive rules can be problematic because they involve subjective value judgements being made. Who decides what is right or wrong? Which model of language do they base it on? What makes the variety of English spoken by one group of people intrinsically better than that of another group?

Descriptive rules, on the other hand, describe how language is actually used. This allows for more variation. A descriptive account may analyse the contexts in which speakers and writers choose to use *less* with a countable noun (*less than eight items*), for example, and may try to explain the circumstances in which this is likely to occur, rather than dismissing it as simply 'wrong'.

For teaching purposes, grammar rules need to be fairly concise because learners are likely to forget lengthy explanations. The rules also need to be fairly simple to understand. This can lead to compromises having to be made in the accuracy of the statements about language. 'Rules' in language teaching are seldom without exceptions and frequently teachers, as learners progress, see a need to modify and extend the rules previously given because they judge that their learners need slightly more sophisticated accounts of the language they encounter. In reality, 'rules' are not so much rules as general guidelines on **typical** language use.

Ways of presenting grammar

In Chapter 4 we saw the need to involve learners and the need to present language in context. We will now look at more ways of presenting grammar.

After each example, read the commentary on page 47.

Classroom example 1

The teacher asks the learners: 'When you were a child, what games did you like playing? Who did you play with?' (Learners may talk in pairs or small groups, or to the teacher.)

Then the teacher gives out the short text below and says: 'Read this short text. What game did Mario play? Who did he play with?'

> Mario: I have very happy memories of being a child. We used to play football nearly every night after school. It was great. My parents hardly ever saw me! I used to go to my friend Carlo's house and play in his garden. Sometimes he came to my house and when he did my mum used to make cakes for us.

Next, the teacher checks the answers to the questions set above and then asks the learners to work in pairs to answer the following questions:

What phrase means 'this happened in the past but not now'?
Underline all the examples of this phrase that you can find.
What sort of word is the phrase followed by?
Does Mario still play football every night?
Did he play football once or many times?
Complete the rule:
We used to play football every night.
____ to + ____ expresses a past _____ which is not done now.

The teacher moves around the room and helps where necessary. She then confirms the answers with the whole class and explains any difficulties.

1 Answer the grammar questions the teacher asked the class.

2 Is the language presented in context?

3 To what extent does the teacher tell the class about the new language and to what extent do the learners discover the rules of form and use for themselves?

Classroom example 2

The teacher says: 'Look at this picture.' [Teacher holds up a picture of a dilapidated house.] 'What's wrong with the house?' The teacher elicits some suggestions (these could be prompted by saying such things as 'Tell me about the roof'). 'Would you like to live here? Why not? OK, well my friend, Ronald, bought this house a few months ago and look at it now!' [Teacher holds up a picture of the same house but beautifully restored.] 'But Ronald isn't a builder – he paid a builder to work on the house. Now tell me what has happened to the windows. He....' [Teacher tries to elicit the sentence *'He has had the windows replaced'*]. If necessary, the teacher gives one example and then asks for others which follow the same pattern.

4 In this example, do the learners talk to each other in groups or to the whole class?

5 Do you think the teacher will write any examples on the board?

Classroom example 3

The teacher brainstorms the names of some famous people with the class. The teacher then tells the class that the government has decided to create a new public holiday, which will be named after a famous person. The learners are the committee who will decide who the day should be named after. The learners work in groups to nominate one person. Each group must then prepare a brief account of the life of the person that they wish to nominate. When this is completed, each group makes a brief presentation in support of their nominee, and the class votes on who the holiday should be named after. Before the learners start their discussions, the teacher plays a tape to the class of a brief presentation made by a native speaker on the same subject.

After the decision is made, the teacher uses the board to highlight some examples of very good language use, and also some mistakes, which she asks the learners to try to correct themselves. The teacher focuses particularly on the use of past forms.

6 In what way(s) is this way of teaching new language significantly different to the others described?

There are various ways of teaching grammar and teachers need to decide on strategies that are appropriate for their learners. They also need to remember that some items of language may be used in particular contexts and learners need to be aware of any such 'restrictions' in the use of a piece of language. For example, some things may be more common in speech than writing, or may be particularly formal, or direct and so on. For example, 'I was wondering if I could...?' is used in slightly different contexts to 'Can I...?' This should be reflected in the contexts in which the teacher chooses to present the language and may also be more overtly pointed out to the learners where necessary.

To sum up, learners need to have seen new language in context and know:

- how a piece of language is formed
- what it (typically) means
- how it is (typically) used

Ways of practising grammar

Classroom example 1

The teacher gives each student a piece of paper with ten instructions. They all start with 'Find someone who...' and are followed by such things as:

can swim
can speak three or more languages
can play a musical instrument

Find someone who...
can swim
can speak three or more languages
can play a musical instrument
can...

The learners move around the room asking each other questions, such as 'Can you swim?' If the answer is 'Yes', they write the name of the person on the piece of paper next to the appropriate prompt. They must try to collect as many different names as possible. After they have finished the teacher conducts feedback on what they found out and also draws attention to any mistakes she heard.

1 What language does this example practise?

2 Can you think of any other pieces of language which could be practised using the same activity with different prompts?

Classroom example 2

See example 2 in **Ways of presenting grammar**, above. The teacher elicits a sentence such as 'He has had the roof repaired'. The whole class repeats it together. The teacher nominates two or three individuals to repeat it. And then says, 'the windows'. A student responds with a sentence using the same pattern ('He has had the windows replaced'). Again there is repetition of the sentence. The teacher continues with further prompts.

3 Does this activity focus on form or meaning?

Classroom example 3

The teacher talks to the class briefly about her life. She then puts the learners into small groups and asks them to tell each other about their pasts and encourages them to ask each other questions. Later the teacher asks two or three of the students to report back to the class what they found out about their partners. She then highlights examples of good language use and also some mistakes.

4 Does this activity focus on form or meaning?

When teaching new bits of language one of the most important considerations is to provide plenty of varied practice. Typically, the more new language is integrated with existing language the harder the activity tends to be. There is no one correct sequence for practice activities. The teacher needs to be sensitive to the needs of the class. Sometimes it is better to move quickly on to a communicative activity, such as example 3, above, because it will challenge and interest the class. If they find it difficult, the teacher can always go back and provide more consolidation work. On other occasions, classes may require plenty of preparation before they are able to do such a task, and working through other activities beforehand can provide this.

It is likely that in each of the practice activities described above that the teacher had a clear idea of exactly what language would be practised. However, grammar need not always be practised in such discrete units. Indeed, there is integration with other language in example 3, above, and to some extent nearly all speaking activities have the potential to practise grammar, depending on how the teacher deals with the language produced. Here is another activity which practises grammar but less overtly than some of the activities previously described.

Classroom example 4

The teacher tells the class a story, using the following notes:

> A man woke up – found his BMW had been stolen – police couldn't find it – insurance company paid him the money to buy a replacement – few weeks later, saw an advert for a second hand BMW in local paper – seemed a bargain and was less than the money paid him by insurance company – went to see it – surprised – it was his car!

After hearing the story the learners are given a written version but with only the first and last letters of each word given. They work in groups to reconstruct the text. The teacher can help by retelling (or reading) the story at intervals.

A m_n w__e up o_e m_____g a_d f___d t__t h_s BMW h_d b__n s____n. He r______d it to t_e p____e b_t t__y c____'t f__d it. H_s i_______e c_____y p__d h_m t_e m___y to b_y a r_________t. A f_w w___s l___r he s_w an a________t in h_s l___l n_______r f_r a BMW. It s____d an a______e b_____n a_d w_s a______y l__s m___y t__n he h_d r_____d f__m t_e i_____e c______y. So, he w__t to s_e it a_d w_s s_______d to f__d t__t it w_s h_s o_n c_r!

Choosing what grammar to teach

Having concluded that in most teaching contexts grammar should be taught and looked at ways of achieving this, we will now briefly look at selecting grammar to teach.

Look at the following factors that may affect a teacher's choice. Tick the ones that you feel are important.

- [ ] Teach 'easy' things first and gradually build up to more difficult.

- [ ] Teach grammar patterns that are used frequently.
- [ ] Teach the grammar patterns that learners make mistakes with.
- [ ] Teach the grammar patterns that will help learners to say the things they want to say.
- [ ] Teach the next grammar pattern in the course book you are using.

When you are ready, read the commentary on page 48.

Timelines

In Chapter 4 we looked at ways of checking that learners had understood. One suggested technique was to ask short questions. For example:

She's been working here for ages.

Did she start work here in the past, or is she starting now? Does she still work here?

The teacher may also want to ask 'What is 's short for?' to differentiate between *is* and *has* and to help clarify the form.

Another way of checking understanding, or to explain new language, is to use timelines. Timelines are simple diagrams that show how units of language relate to time. Therefore it is a technique which is useful when explaining verb forms but not other aspects of grammar, or vocabulary or pronunciation. Some learners find such a visual stimulus very useful. Look at the example *He used to walk to work.* We can say that this is an action that happened in the past and didn't just happen once but happened repeatedly. Therefore this could be represented by the following timeline:

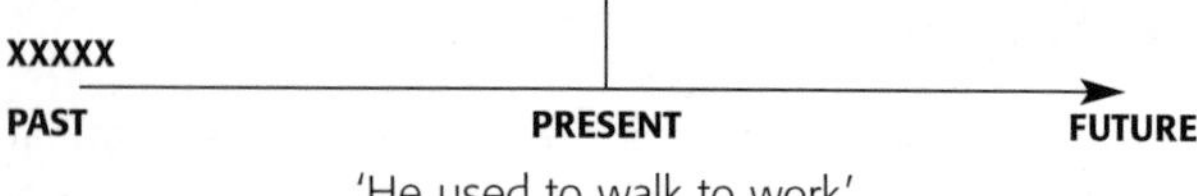

'He used to walk to work.'

Match the following examples with the timelines that follow:

A: *He usually wakes up at about 6.30.*
B: *I'll have been working there for 6 months by Christmas.*
C: *Graham has done a bungee jump.*

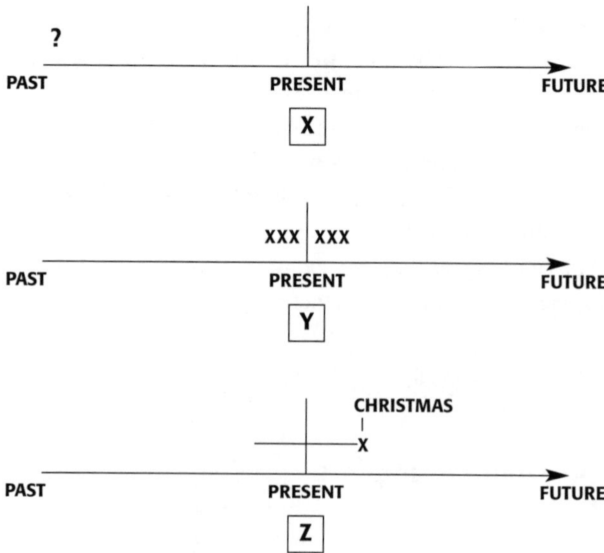

When you are ready, check your answer on page 48.

How would you represent *I've been working here for three years* on a timeline?

When you are ready, check your answer on page 48.

There is no single way of drawing timelines. However, teachers should try to be consistent in the conventions they use with a class, and also explain those conventions. As learners become familiar with the use of timelines, so they can be encouraged to create their own.

Summary

- Teaching grammar involves identifying patterns and their meanings.
- Both form and meaning should be taught.
- Learners generally expect to be taught some grammar.
- Grammar should be presented in a context.
- Grammar should be selected that will be useful to the learners.
- Teachers need to check that learners have understood.
- Teachers should provide the learners with lots of practice opportunities.

CHAPTER

6 Commentary

Ways of presenting grammar

Classroom example 1

1 *Used to* + infinitive of the verb
Mario does not still play football.
Several times – it was a repeated action in the past.
Used to + infinitive expresses a past habit which is not done now.

Note: This structure can also be used to express a past state: *I used to live in Athens.*

2 Yes – the short text provides a context for the language.
3 The teacher supplies the examples of natural language use and provides a framework for the learners to guide their activity. However, to a large extent the learners have to process the language to work out the rule – hopefully leading to better assimilation than if they had simply been told the pattern and its associated meaning.

Classroom example 2

4 The teacher conducts the lesson with the whole class.
5 In the description given the teacher has created a context (the house needing repair) and has elicited the form. She will almost certainly write an example on the board at a later stage so that the learners can see the pattern and it can be highlighted. For example:

He	had	the windows	replaced
subject	auxiliary verb 'have'	object	past participle of the main verb

Classroom example 3

6 In this example communication is prioritised. The learners try to use whatever language they have at their disposal to complete the activity. The teacher listens and after the activity guides the learners to see how they could improve on what they said. There is less of an assumption that a teacher can provide input to the learner on a grammar point and then expect immediate, appropriate and successful 'output' from the learner. Instead, the teacher creates a situation in which learners have the opportunity to use language, and the teacher helps them to notice the differences between their language use and a more expert model. It is argued that such noticing will help learners to develop their own internal awareness of grammar and will eventually lead to successful output.

Ways of practising grammar

Classroom example 1

1 This example practises the use of the modal verb 'can' to express ability. The learners practise the affirmative, negative and interrogative (question) forms.
2 There is a large range of language that could be practised. For example, 'would like', 'used to', the present perfect – the list could go on and on!

Classroom example 2

3 This activity focuses on form. The learners practise saying the words accurately. This may build confidence and help the learners to produce the pattern more automatically, and reduce the need for thought or hesitation.

Classroom example 3

4 This activity focuses mainly on meaning.

Classroom example 4

A man woke up one morning and found that his BMW had been stolen. He reported it to the police but they couldn't find it. His insurance company paid him the money to buy a replacement. A few weeks later he saw an advertisement in his local newspaper for a BMW. It seemed an absolute bargain and was actually less money than he had received from the insurance company. So, he went to see it and was surprised to find that it was his own car!

Choosing what grammar to teach

These considerations can be difficult to separate and a mixture of these may affect the teacher's choice of what to do with a class.

Teach 'easy' things first and gradually build up to more difficult.
Most course books set out to 'grade' grammar in this way and it makes sense to do so. However, it should be remembered that some grammar tends to be learned over time and teachers will probably have to move on to new bits of language before learners have totally mastered the first piece. Language acquisition is often slow and teachers may have to be prepared to go backwards and revise as well as move on.

Teach grammar patterns that are used frequently.
Again, this makes sense. There is little point in spending time on points of grammar that the learners will rarely come across or have a need to use.

Teach the grammar patterns that learners make mistakes with.
This is a useful criterion. Clearly you have to keep in mind the whole class, but if you notice that several members of a group are making similar mistakes with a piece of language, it would be sensible to teach a lesson on this.

Teach the grammar patterns that will help learners to say the things they want to say.
Again, this is a very useful criterion and is related to the above point.

Teach the next grammar pattern in the course book you are using.
In reality this is what dictates the syllabus in many teaching contexts. It is a sensible enough strategy, although each grammar point should be evaluated in the light of the above factors – and overwhelmingly – will it be useful?

Timelines

AY – the Xs signify actions and this is a repeated action.
BZ – the action started in the past and will continue into the future.
CX – the question mark indicates that the action happened in the past, but we don't know exactly when in the past.

I've been working here for three years.
There may be variations but the following would be suitable because the action started three years ago and is still ongoing:

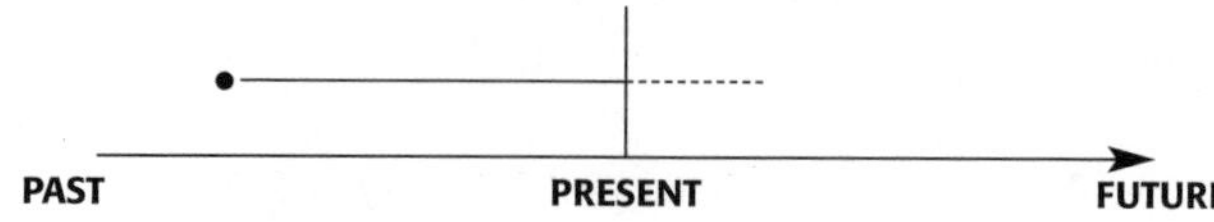

'I've been working here for three years.'

CHAPTER 7

Teaching pronunciation

What is meant by 'pronunciation'?

For our purposes, we will define **pronunciation** as the sounds of the language. The sounds may occur in isolation, or as part of a longer stream of sounds. Like grammar and vocabulary, we can detect patterns in the way the sounds are organised and also the meanings they carry. Like grammar and vocabulary, practice is an essential part of improvement.

Nearly every speech sound is produced by air being pushed from the chest and eventually out through the mouth. The sounds of one language may not correspond exactly to the sounds of another and learners will typically find that the sounds that are new for them are harder to produce than those they already know from their own language.

However, pronunciation is about more than just individual sounds. Learners also need to know which part of a word is stressed. Do we say **Eng**lish or Eng**lish**? As well as the stress of individual words, learners need to realise that where they place the stress in an utterance can also affect its meaning. Intonation, whether the voice moves up or down, is also important. In this chapter we will look at the teaching of each of these aspects of pronunciation in turn.

Pronunciation teaching is often focused on the production of sounds. While this may be very important, there is another aspect of pronunciation teaching which needs to be considered. Learners have to understand the pronunciation used by others. They need to recognise and interpret intonation patterns, subtleties of stress patterns and so on. Teaching learners to recognise and understand the pronunciation of others will help enormously with their ability to listen effectively, and the models may later feed into their own production of language.

Before we consider how to teach pronunciation, we will consider a more fundamental question – do we need to bother to teach pronunciation or can we leave learners to pick it up for themselves?

Do we need to teach pronunciation?

It is possible to make an argument that learners will simply pick up an ability to pronounce words and phrases accurately without having to be taught. In some cases, particularly where a learner is exposed to a lot of natural language, this may indeed be the case. However, the same argument could be made for almost all aspects of language and if learners choose to attend a language course it seems reasonable to assume that they expect to be taught rather than left to pick things up for themselves. A communicative approach to teaching places communicative competence at the centre of what needs to be achieved, and poor pronunciation can impede communication very quickly. This need to develop communicative ability is a strong argument for teaching both receptive and productive aspects of pronunciation. Also, a learner who is aware that their pronunciation is quite good may grow in confidence and then perform better in other aspects of speaking, such as maintaining fluency. The converse may be true for learners who perceive their own pronunciation to be poor.

We need to remember, however, that communicative competence does not imply a native speaker-like competence. The majority of learners will never sound like native speakers and there is no reason why they should. Many learners rarely speak to native speakers but need to use English to speak to other non-native speakers, using English as a common language. Learners should aim to become easily intelligible and to speak with a reasonably natural rhythm so that no undue burden is placed on the person they are speaking to. There are few obvious benefits in them sounding exactly like a native speaker.

Some teachers (both native and non-native speakers) worry about teaching pronunciation because they perceive themselves as having a strong accent. This idea tends to be based on the idea that there is a prestige form of English (usually considered to be something akin to the pronunciation of a traditional BBC presenter) which is in some way better than other forms of English. However, there is nothing about a particular variety of English which makes it intrinsically better than any other and therefore teachers should concern themselves with providing a natural model of English, rather than worrying about which model that is.

Assuming that a teacher decides that s/he needs to teach pronunciation, there is another question that then needs to be addressed. Should teachers plan separate pronunciation lessons or should pronunciation be incorporated into other lessons – those dealing with vocabulary, grammar, speaking and other skills?

Part of the answer to this will depend on the degree of priority that the teacher gives to pronunciation teaching, and this in turn will be dependent on the needs of the learners. Pronunciation teaching should almost certainly be included in other types of lesson, but in many cases separate lessons may be useful as well.

Basic principles

As we have already said, there are different aspects of pronunciation and we will look at each in turn in the following sections. However, first we will briefly look at some principles in teaching pronunciation, which will be useful whatever aspect is being dealt with.

Learners will probably end up copying what they hear. It is therefore important that they hear lots of natural sounding English. Teachers who slow their delivery down too much sometimes deprive their learners of this.

Before trying to get learners to produce the correct sounds, it can be useful to help them to hear the differences between sounds. For example, help learners to recognise the difference between /p/ and /b/, intonation rises and falls and also to recognise where stress is placed.

One problem for learners hearing differences is that pronunciation features are so transitory. Making pronunciation visual creates the possibility of a permanent record. This may be done by transcribing individual sounds, or by marking stress patterns on new items of vocabulary, or by indicating common intonation patterns on new features of language when they are written on the board. Seeing the difference between forms can help learners move towards hearing the difference, and eventually to producing the difference.

As we saw with grammar and vocabulary, practice is very important, so give learners the opportunity to say the word, or sequence of words, several times.

Just as with any other part of language, correction is a useful way of helping learners to improve their pronunciation. However, learners often feel self conscious about their pronunciation, and it is therefore important for teachers to be sensitive while correcting students and to remain very encouraging. (See Chapter 13.)

Here is a summary of some generally useful tips on teaching pronunciation:

- give lots of exposure to natural spoken English
- help learners to hear differences before producing differences
- make pronunciation teaching visual where possible
- give lots of practice
- use (sensitive) correction

Using phonemic symbols

Phonemic symbols are used to transcribe the sounds of a given language. By convention they are written between slanting lines – /k/ /ɑː/ and so on. Words and phrases follow the same convention – so 'car' is represented by /kɑː/, for example.

Phonetic symbols can be used to transcribe the sounds found in all human languages and are typically written between square brackets [ ]. For our purposes we need only think of phonemic symbols because this book is dealing with the teaching of English.

Teachers often have mixed feelings about using the symbols with learners. On the one hand the symbols allow learners to make a written record of sound, which is useful to take away. The symbols can help with effective dictionary use because learners can see how words are pronounced as well as spelt. Some learners can find it difficult to detect a difference between two similar sounds and it is often easier to see the difference when the word is transcribed. Phonemic symbols, when known to learners, can also be used very effectively to correct pronunciation mistakes.

On the other hand, teachers sometimes feel that the additional learning burden placed on students outweighs these advantages. In making their decision teachers need to consider the priorities of their learners, their expectations, and the length of the course, as well as a range of other factors. One compromise is to teach just the symbols which represent the sounds that a particular group of learners finds difficult. Three or four symbols will be fairly quick to teach, but if well chosen may cover a fairly high proportion of the difficulties that learners have.

For a list of the phonemic symbols commonly used to transcribe English, see Appendix 3.

Connected speech

When people speak quite quickly and produce a stream of words, there is often an effect on how individual words sound. Small changes can occur in how words are pronounced when compared to how they may be pronounced in isolation. It is important that learners are not distracted by these changes when listening. Some teachers feel that learners should be taught to produce these features of speech, as well as understand them, because this can lead to learners speaking with a more natural rhythm. On the other hand, some teachers feel that learners do not need to concern themselves with such details and will pick up many of the features automatically. However, it is important that teachers at least produce natural models of speech which include these features, so that learners become familiar with them.

Below is a very brief summary of some of the main features of connected speech. Some of this may seem complicated but remember, teachers may not wish to overtly teach all these features. If teachers do want to introduce some of this to learners, then weak forms may be the most straightforward and useful for students to work on first.

Weak forms

In English we tend to stress the words that are important to the message. Look at the following utterances. Try saying them aloud and think of the pronunciation of *of*, *but* and *and*.

a bucket of sand

salt and pepper
last but not least

Of, *and* and *but* are not usually stressed in these utterances. Several words in English have both a strong and weak form – the strong form is when it is stressed and the weak form when it is not. The forms are different in that in the weak form the vowel sound is reduced. In spoken English weak forms are exceptionally common and contribute to learners being able to speak with a reasonably natural rhythm.

Often the vowel is reduced to a 'schwa' sound which is represented in the phonemic chart by /ə/. It occurs in many unstressed syllables and is the most common vowel sound in English. Even if you do not wish to teach all symbols in the phonemic chart, this one may be worth teaching as it is problematic for many learners and can affect their ability to use word stress and utterance stress appropriately.

Linking sounds

When two vowel sounds occur together there is often a linking sound which comes between them. For example: 'My', said in isolation, would probably be produced as /maɪ/ and 'old' as /əʊld/.
However, when they are said together a /j/ sound typically comes between them – /maɪ(j)əʊld/.
Similarly, a /w/ sound intrudes between the vowel sound of 'too' and the first vowel sound in 'expensive', so 'too expensive' would probably be said as /tuː(w)ɪkˈspensɪv/.
A /r/ sound is likely to occur between the end of 'law' and the first sound of 'and' so that 'law and order' becomes /lɔː(r) ənd ˈɔːdə/.

Elision

Sometimes sounds are missed out altogether. In 'Humpty Dumpty sat on a wall…' the /p/ is often missed out. Elision is common where three consonants come together – the middle one is often dropped.

Coalescence

When a /t/ sound is followed by a /j/ sound, they often blend to form a /tʃ/ sound.
*Don'****t*** *you just love….?*

When a /d/ sound is followed by a /j/ sound, they often blend to form a /dʒ/ sound.
*Di****d*** *you hear what he said to her?*

Assimilation

Those consonants formed using the alveolar ridge (the bony ridge just behind the top front teeth – feel where your tongue touches when you produce a /t/ sound) sometimes change in connected speech. For example, 'whiteboard' may be produced as something more like 'wipeboard' because the /b/ sound which follows changes what would have been an alveolar sound.

Teaching activities

1 Give the learners a short tapescript. Ask them where they think there will be a linking sound, a weak form, or other feature of connected speech. Learners listen to the tape to see if they were correct. If you want to focus on production, ask learners to practise and then record their efforts at reading the tapescript.

2 Read sentences fairly quickly. Ask the learners to count how many words they hear. Contractions, such as 'I'm' count as two words. This is good for helping learners to perceive weak forms and the way in which words are linked.

Individual sounds

Vowels and consonants

The sounds of a language can be analysed in great detail but for our purposes we will look at three broad categories of sounds. A pure vowel sound is created when the air stream remains relatively unobstructed. The pronunciation of the /ɪ/ sound in 'sit' or the /iː/ sound in 'seat' are examples. A diphthong is created when there is a movement (or 'glide') from one vowel sound to another. The /eɪ/ sound in 'eight' is an example. Consonant sounds are produced when the teeth, lips, tongue and so on are used to restrict air flow in various ways. The /p/ and /b/ sounds in 'pub' are examples – the lips restrict the airflow before it is released.

It should be noted that the words 'vowel' and 'consonant' here are used to refer to sounds, not letters. There are only five vowel letters in English but twenty pure vowel and diphthong sounds.

Where sounds in English correspond to sounds in the mother tongue of the student, they can generally be produced with little or no difficulty. Where a mother tongue has a sound similar to that in English, this may get substituted in place of the English sound. The degree to which this is likely to affect communication depends on the context in which it occurs.

Voiced and unvoiced sounds

Look at the following sounds. Put them into pairs according to the position of the lips, teeth and tongue when making them. What is different about the way in which the sounds in each pair are produced?
/s/ /z/ /t/ /v/ /d/ /f/

When you are ready, read the commentary on page 56.

Teaching activities

1 Sometimes sounds can be taught by the teacher modelling the sound and having learners repeat it. However, sometimes this is not enough to allow learners to create sounds, particularly those that are completely new to them, and the teacher needs to use a more mechanical approach. One such approach is to tell the students how to make sounds.

Match the sounds on the left with the descriptions of how to make them on the right.

/f/	**1** put your tongue just behind your top front teeth and very close to the roof of your mouth. Squeeze the air out.
/s/	**2** put your tongue on the bony ridge just behind the front top teeth, blocking the air stream completely before releasing it
/t/	**3** gently bite the bottom lip as you squeeze the air out.

When you are ready, check your answers on page 56.

Write a similar description on how to pronounce the 'th' in the word 'thin'.

When you are ready, check your answers on page 56.

2 To practise the difference between particular sounds write three or four pairs of words that only differ in that one respect. For example:

/ɪ/	/iː/
grin ship sit bit	green sheep seat beat

Dictate one of the words in each pair and ask the learners to circle the word they hear. To practise production, learners can dictate to each other.

Word stress

The rules governing word stress in English are extremely complicated, and it is doubtful that learning detailed rules will be useful for many learners. However, teachers may think that a few general guidelines may be useful and learners will almost certainly benefit from learning where the stress is placed on each item as they encounter it.

Look at the following list of words. Mark where the primary stress falls on each of them.
camera
photographer
tripod
develop
album

When you are ready, check your answers on page 56.

Consider the following pieces of advice on helping learners with word stress. Which ones do you think are a good idea?

1 When you write new words on the board, indicate where the stress is placed.

2 Ask learners to repeat words after you teach them.

3 Teach learners the conventions used to indicate word stress in dictionaries.

When you are ready, read the commentary on page 56.

Teaching activities

1 Ask the learners to copy the following table from the board.

First syllable	Second syllable	Third syllable

Dictate a series of recently learned words and ask the learners to write them in the appropriate column, according to where the stress falls.

2 Write as many recently learned words as you have learners. Give each learner a piece of paper with one word on. The learners must form themselves into groups according to where the stress is placed on their word. So, for example, all the learners who have a word where the stress falls on the second syllable gather together.

3 Odd one out. Write four words on the board – three should all follow the same stress pattern and one should be different. Ask the learners which one is the 'odd one out'. For example:

flattering fingertip flamboyant following

('Flamboyant' is different because the stress is on the second syllable.) The learners need to be familiar with the words used.

Utterance stress

Utterance stress, or sentence stress as it is sometimes called, refers to where the stress, or stresses, fall when a stream of words is spoken.

For most utterances there is a 'natural', or 'unmarked', way of saying them. For example, in the question 'Where do you live?' there would normally be two stresses, one on the word 'where' and one on 'live'. However, in some circumstances a stress may be placed on one of the other words, but this will affect the meaning. For example:

Becky: *My sister lives in Spain, my brother in France and my mother is in Italy.*
Ian: *And where do **you** live?*
Becky: *Me? In Southampton.*

The following utterance can be said in different ways. Match the way it is said with the meanings that follow.

1 **Most** of the doctors in the hospital were moved to different departments.

2 Most of the **doctors** in the hospital were moved to different departments.

3 Most of the doctors in the hospital were moved to **different** departments.

A The doctors were moved, not the nurses.
B The doctors were not all moved to the same department.
C Not all the doctors were affected.

When you are ready, check your answer on page 56.

Teaching activities

1 Ask the learners how shifting the stress in the utterance affects meaning – as in the doctors/hospital example above.

2 Write a sentence on the board. Ask the learners which words are the most important in conveying the meaning. Read the sentence together, with half the class shouting the important words, and the other half saying the other words quite quickly and quietly.

Intonation

Intonation refers to the patterns of pitch movement, or the 'melody' of the language. The rules governing intonation patterns in English are exceptionally complicated and even many linguists disagree on exactly what the most appropriate analysis is. Again the teacher is left having to judge how useful any 'rules' are, given that there are almost bound to be many exceptions. However, there are some rough guidelines that teachers can give to learners.

As with other aspects of language, any analysis needs to consider the form of intonation and the meanings or uses associated with those forms. Look at the following questions and try to work out some of the guidelines that teachers may give learners. If you have little experience of teaching or learning language this may be quite difficult. Making up examples and saying them aloud will help.

1 What will the effect be of talking with very flat intonation (not much movement and a 'monotone' effect)?

2 What is the difference between 'sorry' said with a rising intonation and said with a falling intonation?

3 What is the difference between 'He spoke to her, didn't he?' said with a falling intonation and said with a rising intonation?

4 In the following list, how can you make it sound complete?
apples, grapes, plums, oranges

5 Statements are usually spoken with a falling intonation pattern. True or false?

6 *Yes/No* questions are usually spoken with a falling intonation. True or false?

7 *Who, what, where, when* type questions can be asked with either a rising or a falling intonation. True or False?

8 To show sarcasm or surprise the intonation pattern often rises and then falls. True or false?

When you are ready, check your answers on page 56.

Teaching

Teaching intonation can be very difficult but here are some golden rules:

- Try to keep a natural model of intonation yourself so that learners will be able to copy from you.
- Ensure learners understand that intonation can affect the meaning of what you say and is therefore important.
- When teaching new pieces of language, practise the appropriate intonation pattern with the learners so that they learn intonation as they go along.

Summary

- The various aspects of pronunciation need to be taught, including the **recognition** of pronunciation features.
- Learners should aim to understand others and to be easily understood. This does not necessarily imply native speaker-like perfection.
- Pronunciation teaching can be integrated into most lessons.
- Pronunciation rules are often very complex and the teacher may help most by providing natural models and encouraging learners to copy them.

CHAPTER

7 Commentary

Individual sounds

Voiced and unvoiced sounds

/t/ /d/ /f/ /v/ /s/ /z/

In each case the sound on the left is different to the one on the right in that it is 'voiceless'. This means that the vocal cords do not vibrate. If you place your fingers in your ears and produce each sound you will hear significantly more when you produce the voiced sounds on the right. /k/ and /g/, /θ/ and /ð/, and /ʃ/ and /tʃ/ could also be added to the list.

Teaching activities

/f/ - 3
/s/ - 1
/t/ - 2

Pronunciation of 'th' (as in 'thin'):
Place the tongue between the top and bottom teeth and squeeze the air around it. Do not vibrate vocal cords.

Word stress

camera
pho**tog**rapher
tripod
de**vel**op
album

1 ***When you write new words on the board, indicate where the stress is placed.***
This is a good idea, particularly on those items of vocabulary that learners have problems with pronouncing accurately. Teachers need to establish a clear method for indicating where the stress would fall. One technique is to put a circle or a box over the stressed syllable. It can be a good idea to use a different colour for this from the one in which the word is written so that learners who are trying to understand an alphabet which may be different to their own are not confused.

2 ***Ask learners to repeat words after you teach them.***
This is a useful technique. Sometimes the teacher can reinforce this by tapping the stress pattern on the table.

3 ***Teach learners the conventions used to indicate word stress in dictionaries.***
This is very useful. It is important to remember that different dictionaries may follow different conventions.

Utterance stress

1 C **2** A **3** B

Intonation

1 Very flat intonation can give the impression of boredom or lack of interest. Particularly where an extended speaking turn is taken (such as in a speech or presentation) flat intonation can make it hard for the audience to concentrate and fully engage with what is being said.

2 'Sorry' said with rising intonation is usually a request for repetition of some kind but with a falling pattern it is an apology.

3 This is an example of a question tag. Said with falling intonation it usually means that the speaker is virtually certain that what they are saying is true, but with a rising intonation it sounds more like a genuine question.

4 When listing things, the intonation pattern usually rises when the list is incomplete and there is more to follow and falls on completion.

5 True

6 False – usually with a rising intonation.

7 True – learners are often taught that they are asked with a falling intonation pattern but this is not always the case, particularly if the question is repeated or the questioner believes s/he should already know the answer.

8 True

CHAPTER 8 Developing reading skills

Skills development lessons

Earlier in the book we looked at the systems of vocabulary, grammar and pronunciation and saw how these are important to develop because they contribute to learners performing better when they speak, listen, read and write. However, communicative approaches also emphasise the need to give direct practice in these areas of direct performance. The four skills can be divided into receptive and productive skills as follows:

Productive	Receptive
Speaking Writing	Listening Reading

The receptive skills are so labelled because they are to do with receiving and decoding information. They are certainly not passive skills, as often they require much effort. There is a good deal of overlap in the methodology used in developing the two receptive skills.

Sources of material

Teachers sometimes use texts with learners which were not specifically designed for teaching purposes. For reading skills teachers may use an article from a newspaper or magazine, for example, or an extract from a novel. To develop listening skills they may use a recording from the radio or television. Texts such as these, which were **not** originally written to be used for teaching purposes, are usually referred to as 'authentic texts'. They give exposure to 'real' English and can be very motivating for learners. However, as well as the many advantages to using them, there are also some disadvantages. They can be time consuming for a teacher to prepare (writing appropriate questions and so on), and they can sometimes date quickly, making the time spent in preparation disproportionate to their value. In addition, the level of complexity (particularly the vocabulary load) can make them difficult for lower level learners to process.

Teachers also sometimes use texts which have been specially written for teaching purposes. These can ensure that the text is pitched at an appropriate level for a group and therefore allow for easier processing. However, if they are not well written they can sometimes appear stilted and unnatural, and in these cases their usefulness may be questionable.

Sometimes reading and listening texts can be based on authentic extracts, but be slightly modified to meet the presumed needs of a group.

Whatever the source of the material, reading and listening texts need to be challenging for learners, while still allowing them a good chance to understand the main points. Learners do not need to understand every word (they are unlikely to do this in real life situations) but if there is too much that cannot be understood, learners are likely to become demotivated quite quickly.

Reading in 'real life'

Look at the following examples of reading. Put the nine examples into three groups of three, according to the way in which the texts are likely to be read (quickly, slowly, taking care with each word and phrase, type of information looked for and so on). Note: It may be possible to argue for alternative groupings.

Tracy is looking for a number in a telephone directory.

Rachel is reading the instructions on how to complete her tax return.

Paul is writing his university dissertation and is looking for a quote he needs – he knows it's somewhere in Chapter 7!

Josh is glancing at an old letter from his insurance company to see if he can throw it away.

Nicole is reading the directions of how to get to her holiday destination.

Maria is flicking through a magazine while she waits for the dentist.

Steven is looking through the classified advertisements because he wants to buy a second-hand car for under £1500.

Belinda is reading a detective story, which she's enjoying, although it has a complicated plot.

Richard is in a bookshop and also in a hurry. He's looking at the back of a couple of paperbacks to see which one would make the best present for his girlfriend.

When you have finished, check your answer with the one on page 62.

From the examples above it is important to note two things. First, the people in the examples all have **a reason for reading** – Tracy needs a phone number, Nicole doesn't want to get lost, Richard needs to find out the rough content of the book and so on.

Second, the people read in different ways because they are reading for different reasons.

Richard, Maria and Josh are trying to get a general impression of their text as fast as they can. This is often referred to as **skim reading** or **gist reading**.

Steven, Paul and Tracy are also reading very quickly but are looking for a very specific piece of information. If Steven sees £1950 in the advert he probably doesn't bother reading anything else about that car. This is often referred to as **scan reading**. Scan reading involves looking for a particular word or piece of information.

Belinda, Nicole and Rachel probably concentrate on more or less every word because they need a detailed understanding of the text. This is often referred to as **intensive reading**.

Learners need to develop similarly flexible reading skills – in other words, they need to be able to read quickly to understand the gist of a text, or to find some very specific information, and they also need to be able to read for a more detailed understanding.

Reading in the classroom

Imagine that Belinda is a teacher of an Elementary class. She wants to develop reading skills and decides to give her learners an extract from her detective story to read. She doesn't write any questions but thinks the students will enjoy it anyway.
Do you think this is likely to be a successful lesson? Why/why not?

Steven decides to use his classified advertisements in a lesson. He gives the learners a list of people who all want to buy specified things. The students must try to find what they need in the classified ads Steven has provided.

Later Steven's friend, Alice, asks to borrow the ads for her lesson. However, before giving out the ads she asks

students what sort of things may be advertised there. She then asks them if they have ever bought or sold anything in this way. She allows students to chat about this for a few minutes before completing the same task as Steven used.
Whose lesson is likely to be better and why?

Robin and Nicole use the same reading activity with their classes. The learners read a text and answer some multiple choice questions. At the end of the activity Robin nominates a learner and asks for the answer – 'Maria, what is the answer for number 1?', and so on. Nicole does the same thing, but before doing this asks the learners to compare answers in pairs or small groups for a few moments.
What are the advantages of Nicole's strategy?

When you have thought about these situations, look at the commentary on page 62.

As we have said, students need a reason to read and this can often be achieved in the classroom by setting a meaningful task. Setting questions is a way of focusing learners on the most important parts of a text and therefore helping them to understand it. The students also need to have a chance to think of what they already know about the subject because this too may help them with decoding it.

If there are new words in the text that the learners are unlikely to know, the teacher may also choose to pre-teach a few of them so that the students don't get frustrated and disheartened while reading. However, it is not always necessary to pre-teach vocabulary and the students need practice in dealing with texts where they don't know every word – this is much closer to their real life experience.

An example reading lesson

We will now look at how reading skills could be developed by looking at an example reading lesson.

A: First, think about which animals you think make the best pets.

B: Look at the following words:
blaze, cat flap, nominate (for an award), *gutted* (the house)

You are going to read a newspaper story called 'Fur alarm'. Consider for a few moments what the story may be about.

When you are ready, read the article on page 140 very quickly (2 minutes maximum). Was your prediction correct?

C: Look at the following numbers:
64, 62, 13, 5
Find what they refer to in the text as quickly as possible.

When you are ready, check your answers on page 62.

D: Look at the following questions. Read the text again and answer them.

1 Could Polly have escaped without waking Jean and John?

2 How did Polly wake Jean?

3 How did Jean react to Polly trying to wake her?

4 Why couldn't Jean go downstairs?

5 How did the fire start?

6 Were Jean and John badly hurt?

7 Was Polly badly hurt?

8 In what way is Polly a heroine?

When you are ready, check your answers on page 62.

E: What are the advantages and disadvantages of keeping pets?

Reflection on the lesson

1 Look at sections B, C and D. Which type of reading skill is practised in each section?

2 Why is it a good idea to order the reading activities in this way?

3 Do you think the learners should read silently or aloud? Why?

4 What is the purpose of the final question? ('What are the advantages and disadvantages of keeping pets?') What skills may be practised here?

5 If you were teaching this lesson to a group of students and some of them volunteered the wrong answers, what would you do?

When you are ready, check your answers on page 62.

Stages of a reading or listening lesson

A plan for the above reading lesson can be found on page 110. However, the typical stages that may be used in a reading or listening lesson can be summarised as follows:

- build interest
- pre-teach vocabulary (if necessary)
- set a gist or scanning task
- learners read (or listen)
- learners compare answers
- learners check answers with the teacher
- set an intensive reading (or listening) task
- learners read (or listen)
- learners compare answers
- learners check answers with the teacher
- set an extension activity

This is not the only format reading and listening lessons may take and the teacher may wish to include an extra task (for example by including both gist and scanning tasks), and also by having learners read or listen a further time at the intensive stage. However, the above serves as a general guide.

Developing literacy

In most teaching contexts, learners will have learned to read and write in their own language before attempting to learn English. Even though conventions may vary from culture to culture and language to language, the fact that skills have been learned once, usually results in core skills being transferred to the new language, in this case English, and so the task of learning to read in the target language becomes that much easier.

However, occasionally this is not the case, and teachers have to go back to the basics of teaching reading skills. This means that learners have to become aware of the range of sounds that letters (and combinations of letters) can represent. This 'phonics' approach is often how a child learns to read in their own language. Using this system learners can work out what written words mean (as long as they know the spoken form). Teachers can also help learners to remember whole words from their shapes as this can speed up the reading process and is a particularly useful way of dealing with frequent words.

Here are three activities which may help learners in the early stages of learning to read. Learners who have learned to read and write in their own language but whose language uses a different script, such as Arabic or Chinese, may benefit from similar activities.

1 The teacher shows the class five pictures and checks that they know the spoken form for what is depicted in each picture. The teacher then gives the learners the words in written form and they have to match them to the pictures.

2 The teacher gives the learners five words which have similar written forms. The teacher gives them in both lower and upper case. The learners have to match the lower case example with the equivalent upper case one. For example:

house	HEART
horse	HEAR
hear	HEAD
heart	HOUSE
head	HORSE

3 The teacher distributes a simple text made up of two or three sentences to the learners. The teacher reads the text and the learners try to follow. The teacher stops after every few words and asks 'What's the next word?'.

Summary

- Build interest in a topic before starting the reading.
- Set a task **before** asking the learners to read. Questions help to focus learners on the important parts of texts.
- Consider the advantages of using authentic texts, at least some of the time.
- Consider whether it is necessary to pre-teach any vocabulary.
- Ensure the learners read the text more than once by setting different tasks.
- Generally concentrate on developing silent reading skills rather than reading aloud.

CHAPTER

8 Commentary

Reading in 'real life'

A possible answer:

Richard, Maria, Josh	Steven, Paul, Tracy	Belinda, Nicole, Rachel
all reading quickly but not for anything very specific	*all reading very quickly for a specific piece of information*	*all reading carefully and trying to get a detailed understanding*

Reading in the classroom

For most classes Belinda's idea is probably not a very wise one. The learners have no reason to read this (other than that the teacher has told them to). This contrasts with the 'real life' reading experience we looked at earlier. It's also very likely that there will be too many difficult words in the text for the students to understand very much at all. It is important to remember that the text was originally written for native speakers and Belinda's class is only Elementary level.

Alice's lesson is likely to be better because she has made an effort to build interest in the texts before the students read. Also in 'real life', we usually know something about the topic and genre of what we are going to read (consider the purpose of a newspaper headline) and this helps in the understanding process. Readers can bring their 'real world knowledge' to the text and this is likely to help them to understand it.

One very common technique used by teachers to achieve these things is to ask students to **predict** what they think they will read, based on a picture accompanying the text, the title, some key words, their knowledge of the subject and text type and so on.

Nicole's idea of letting learners compare answers is a good one. For one thing, it builds confidence as learners share ideas before speaking in front of the class. Learners can help each other to find what is correct and why. Comparing also allows for a variety of focus in the lesson as learners speak to each other for a few moments, rather than just to the teacher.

An example reading lesson

B: various answers are possible

C:

64 = John's age
62 = Jean's age
13 = Polly's age
5 = number of minutes before Jean would have died

D:

1 Yes – through the cat flap
2 Polly hit Jean's face with her paw and made a noise.
3 She tried to make her stop.
4 There was too much smoke.
5 There was an electrical problem with the freezer.
6 No.
7 No – but she had breathed in a lot of smoke.
8 She risked her own life to help others.

Reflection on the lesson

1 B is a gist task (also referred to as skim reading). C is a scanning task. D is an intensive reading task.

2 The learners are asked to read the text three times. The first time to get a quick impression of the meaning, content and text type – skim reading. The next task is scan reading – looking for specific bits of information. The third reading task is more intensive in nature, demanding more detailed understanding. There are two reasons to use the first two reading tasks. First, these reading skills are worth practising in their own right because they are frequently used in 'real life' reading. Second, they are designed to help the more intensive reading because the reader already has some understanding of the text and how it is organised. Not all texts lend themselves to developing all three reading subskills developed here. However, it is usually a good idea to give learners a chance to read a text fairly quickly at least once before introducing an intensive reading task.

3 Learners should generally read silently. Reading aloud is not a skill that many people use much in real life and therefore few learners need to practise it to any great extent. Some teachers

argue that by having learners read aloud, they can help with pronunciation. However, even native speakers often have problems with intonation and stress when reading aloud. Pronunciation is generally linked to speaking, rather than reading, and should therefore be practised in that context. Where learners are asked to read aloud, they will benefit from having the opportunity to prepare the text first because they will only be able to place appropriate stress patterns and so on if they understand what they are reading. In teaching contexts where genuine speaking practice is difficult to provide, teachers may decide that reading aloud is the only way they can provide any pronunciation practice.

4 This is an 'extension activity' – introducing speaking and listening skills. This gives variety to the lesson, both in skills focus and also pace, and gives learners the opportunity to make reference to what they have read while practising a different skill. This may help the learner assimilate new information about the topic with what they already knew before reading.

5 Always try to help learners see **why** one answer is better than another. For example, tell learners the part of the text which gives the correct answer. Invite them to re-read it and so on. Always ensure that at the end of the activity all the learners are clear on the correct answers to any task.

CHAPTER

9 Developing listening skills

Reading and listening lessons

In the previous chapter we looked at some of the main considerations in lessons which aim to develop reading skills, and in this chapter will look at some of the features peculiar to listening lessons. Although much of the methodology is common to both types of receptive skill lesson, listening and reading are different. When listening there is often a pressure to respond almost immediately, and also a pressure brought about by having only 'one go' at understanding (unlike reading where you can backtrack and read again). As well as these features, there is also the need to understand intonation patterns, features of fast connected speech and to deal with the possible distractions of background noise.

Here are some of the factors we considered important in a reading lesson. They have been reworded to include both receptive skills. Are all the points relevant to listening lessons?

- The level of the text is important. It should challenge learners without being **too** difficult.
- Teachers need to consider whether there is a need to pre-teach a few items of vocabulary.
- Teachers need to set meaningful tasks before reading/listening to help understanding and to mirror the 'real life' situation of reading/listening for a purpose.
- After reading/listening learners should have the opportunity to compare answers with each other before checking with the teacher.
- Listening/reading skills can be subdivided to include such things as gist understanding (getting an overall idea) or a more detailed understanding.
- Typically learners will read/listen to the same text more than once.
- Teachers should try to build some interest in the text before setting reading/listening tasks.

When you are ready, check your ideas with the commentary on page 68.

Varieties of listening input

Look at the list of activities which involve listening. Tick the ones that you have done in the last 48 hours.

- [ ] made or received a telephone call
- [ ] listened to a radio news bulletin
- [ ] watched a television news bulletin
- [ ] had a conversation with a friend
- [ ] listened to a lecture
- [ ] had a conversation with a group of friends
- [ ] watched a movie either in the cinema or on television
- [ ] watched at least 10 minutes of daytime television
- [ ] listened to a music CD or audio cassette
- [ ] taken part in a small discussion group

Notice again that just as we saw when looking at reading lessons, native speakers always have a reason for listening to something. If we listen to a news bulletin we want to know what is happening in the world. It is likely that we want information from a lecture, and when we speak to friends we want to maintain and build those relationships. This reason for listening needs to be replicated in the classroom. Notice too that some tasks combine the skill of listening with that of speaking. One useful way in which teachers can help learners to listen more effectively is to teach them the skills they need to manage a conversation. Teachers can help learners to develop 'strategies' for coping when they find understanding difficult, by teaching them such things as ways of asking for clarification or indicating that they haven't understood. We will look at examples of this later in the chapter.

Imagine doing the above things in a foreign language. Answer the questions that follow.

1 Which would be harder, listening to the news on the radio or watching it on television? Why?

2 Which would be harder, talking to a friend on the telephone or face to face? Why?

3 Which would be harder, talking to a friend or to a group of friends? Why?

4 How is watching a movie different from watching 10 minutes of daytime television?

5 How is listening to a lecture different from listening to music on a CD?

6 How is listening to a lecture different from taking part in a small discussion group?

When you are ready, read the commentary on page 68.

We can see that native speakers listen in flexible ways according to the contexts in which they are listening. This flexibility and range of skill is something that learners need help developing.

What makes listening difficult

Here are some comments made by learners of English on why they find listening difficult. In each case try to think of a way the teacher could help the situation.

1 I worry more about listening than reading because you can't go back to check. *Cinzia, Italy*

2 English people speak too fast and sometimes the words sound different to the way I learned them. *Alejandra, Chile* (studying in the UK)

3 My school is near the airport. Sometimes the noise of the planes stops me understanding. *Nena, Athens*

4 I can understand my teacher but other people with different accents are really hard for me to understand. *Li Na, China*

5 English people 'eat their words'. *Maria, Madrid*

6 I can understand videos very well but audio tapes are quite difficult for me. *Stefan, Germany*

7 I can understand English people when they speak only to me but I find it hard to join in their conversation. *Anja, Switzerland*

8 I can listen OK for a short time but then I get tired and miss things. *Milena, Brazil*

9 I worry when there is a word I don't understand. *Jacques, France*

10 I remember I was very confused when I started learning English because I didn't know what 'um' and 'er' meant! *Emiliano, Italy*

Helping learners to overcome problems

Look at the list below of some of the things that a teacher can do to help students with listening. Which learner(s) (from the previous section) would each activity help? Some activities may help more than one learner and some learners may be helped in more than one way.

Skills to negotiate meaning

Teach learners ways of asking for repetition ('Sorry, could you repeat that, please?') and also of checking that they are following the speaker ('So, she forgot to pay for the dress?')

Variety of accents

Provide students with examples of different speakers so that they listen to varieties of English other than their teacher. Remember, many people use English to speak to other non-native speakers and so not all the accents need necessarily be from the UK or other English-speaking environments.

Word counting exercises

Read a sentence to the class at normal speed using usual contractions, stress and intonation. The students must count how many words are in the sentence (contractions count as two).

Play the tape more than once

Where tapes are used, it can be a good idea to reassure learners that they will hear the tape again before you first play it. This can help to reduce the stress of listening and this in itself may lead to better performance.

Hesitations and false starts

Occasionally draw students' attention to how native speakers use hesitation devices to create thinking time. Help students to 'filter out' the unneeded parts of spoken English so that they can focus better on the really meaningful parts.

Set achievable/meaningful tasks

Well-set tasks can help learners to focus on the important parts of a text. It can also help them to realise that they can understand the message of the speaker without having to understand every word.

Show learners pictures

This is useful when using audio tapes or other situations when the nature of the input does not provide any visual stimulus.

When you are ready, read the commentary on page 68.

Some practical considerations

The participants on a teacher training course were asked to teach a lesson which was not observed by their tutor. After the lesson they wrote a commentary on what happened. Read the extracts from the commentaries and answer the questions.

Jon:
I tried to play the tape a second time for the students but I couldn't find the right place on the tape – I think I rewound it too far – so I read it to them instead.

1 How could Jon have ensured he found the right place?

2 Do you think that reading the text was a good idea in the circumstances?

Judith:
I played the tape and then asked the learners a few questions. Most of the students did OK.

3 What advice would you give Judith?

Laura:
I told the students they would hear the tape twice, but they found it quite difficult and hadn't really understood, so I ended up playing it three times.

4 Was Laura right to tell her students how many times they were going to listen?

5 Was she right to change her plan?

Andy:
While the learners were listening to the tape I wrote the vocabulary they needed for the next activity on the board to save time.

6 Do you think this was a good idea?

Kirsty:
Before I asked the students for their answers I got them to check in pairs. I could see they all had different answers so I played the tape again and stopped it in two or three places.

7 Do you think Kirsty was right to play the tape again?

8 Was she right to stop the tape?

Rachel:
We've listened to a lot of tapes recently so I wanted to do something a bit different. I wrote a story about something that really happened to me and read it to the class.

9 Do you like Rachel's idea for a listening lesson?

10 Can you think of any ways of adapting it?

Mike:
As the learners watched a television documentary about becoming an astronaut, they made notes.

11 What assumptions would you make about the level of Mike's class?

Tracy:
We watched a video of a news summary. Before listening I asked students what was in the news at the moment. The first task was to put stories in order as they listened – foreign news, sports news, weather, politics and so on.

12 What type of listening skill was the first task practising – intensive listening or gist listening?

When you are ready, check your answers in the commentary on page 69.

Summary

- The receptive skills of listening and reading have much in common.
- People listen to various types of input and learners need exposure to varied material and tasks.
- It is important to empower learners while they listen, by giving them the language to ask for clarification, repetitions, and request a slower delivery.
- Try to help learners appreciate how much they **do** understand rather than always focus on what they didn't manage to grasp.

CHAPTER

9 Commentary

Reading and listening lessons

All the points are relevant to both types of lesson.

Varieties of listening input

1 ***Which would be harder, listening to the news on the radio or watching it on television? Why?***
Typically people tend to find that listening to the radio is more difficult than watching television. This is because television can support the message visually. In the case of the news, there may be maps, captions at the top or bottom of the screen, tables of figures and so on.

2 ***Which would be harder, talking to a friend on the telephone or face to face? Why?***
Typically the telephone conversation is judged to be harder (although the topic of the conversation may affect this). The reasons are similar to those above – the degree of visual support. In the case of face-to-face interaction, this is usually in the form of body language of some kind.

3 ***Which would be harder, talking to a friend or to a group of friends? Why?***
People generally judge that it is harder to talk to a group of friends than an individual in a foreign language. This may be because an individual is more likely to make concessions and adapt their speech to be understood. It is also because the turn-taking (when you should speak) is easier to manage in a one-to-one conversation.

4 ***How is watching a movie different from watching 10 minutes of daytime television?***
A movie demands much greater attention and for a longer period of time. Also it is usually important to follow the story from start to finish whereas daytime television tends to change topic quite regularly, giving the listener a fresh start and a new chance to understand.

5 ***How is listening to a lecture different from listening to music on a CD?***
A lecture may not be for pleasure – there may also be the added burden of taking notes while listening.

6 ***How is listening to a lecture different from taking part in a small discussion group?***
Lectures rarely demand interaction whereas the listener will also be expected to take turns as a speaker in the discussion group.

Helping learners to overcome problems

Skills to negotiate meaning
Generally useful and will probably benefit everyone. This is a way of giving students some control over the listening process and can therefore make listening less stressful.

Variety of accents
Again, this is generally useful and would certainly benefit Li Na.

Word counting exercises
This can be a useful way of helping learners to perceive and understand unstressed words and the way in which words join together. It would particularly help Maria, as it is the way in which we link words in rapid speech that leads to the impression that we 'eat our words'. This may explain part of Alejandra's problem that the words sound different to how she learned them. Sometimes in natural (fairly quick speech) sounds can be dropped from words, extra sounds added as we link words, or sounds may change slightly. One way to help learners with these phenomena is to ensure that they get plenty of practice in listening to natural language.

Play the tape more than once
This would help Cinzia and perhaps Milena.

Hesitations and false starts
This would have helped Emiliano.

Set achievable/meaningful tasks
Again, this is generally useful and would certainly help Jacques.

Show learners pictures
This would help Stefan.

Some practical considerations

1 Assuming the tape recorder had a counter, Jon should have used it.

2 In the circumstances he had little alternative. Some texts can be read aloud without too much trouble (particularly when only one voice is needed) but dialogues, for example, are much harder. Remember also that learners need to hear a variety of accents and not just the teacher's.

3 Set the task before listening so that you know that you can focus learners on key parts of the text. Setting questions after listening can become a test of memory.

4 Generally it is a good idea to tell students how many times they will hear the tape.

5 Sometimes it is necessary to change your plan and it is good to be responsive to the needs of the people you are teaching.

6 This is not a good idea because it can be very distracting. Learners need to focus fully on what they are listening to.

7 One of the advantages of allowing students to check in pairs is that you can gather this type of information and Kirsty did well to respond to it.

8 Having realised that the students found the listening task quite difficult, this was a sensible strategy to make the task more achievable.

9 This is potentially a nice activity.

10 Spoken English is different in many ways to written English – there is repetition, false starts, hesitations and so on. It may have been a good idea just to tell the story rather than read it – perhaps using a few notes. Rachel could ask a colleague to tell a story so that learners hear a variety of accents.

11 Combining listening and writing is very difficult so we could conclude that Mike's class is quite a high level. At lower levels learners need to be set tasks that allow them to concentrate solely on listening (ticking boxes, etc.) and which do not demand other language skills.

12 Gist listening because the learners only need to work out the topic, not the detail of the story. Notice that Tracy sets the activity up and builds some interest before playing the tape.

CHAPTER

10 Developing writing skills

We have looked at the receptive skills of reading and listening. This chapter will look at the productive skill of writing, but first we will consider the ways in which writing is different to speech.

Differences between writing and speech

There are some clear distinctions between writing and speaking. However, we should remember that most of the distinctions below are based on typical samples of writing and typical samples of speech. Of course, there is writing which resembles speech (something a script writer would try to master) and some writing may become spoken language (a political speech, or news broadcast, for example). Therefore texts can be placed on a continuum, with typically written texts (for example, formal academic writing) at one end and typically spoken texts (such as chatting to friends) at the other. How we write and speak will depend on the context in which we are writing and speaking (who to, the topic and so on). E-mails have features of both written and spoken language, as well as containing features that belong to neither speech nor writing!

Look at the characteristics below. For each one indicate whether you associate it with writing ('W') or speech ('S'). The first two have been done as examples. Are there any statements that you disagree with?

1 It develops automatically in healthy children. (S)

2 It is taught to children later in their development. (W)

3 It is used with physical movements, such as gestures.

4 There is a time constraint – you need to produce language quite quickly.

5 There is typically little or no time constraint.

6 Accuracy is expected.

7 There is a greater tolerance of inaccuracy.

8 The language produced is not always organised into 'complete sentences'.

9 There is a high degree of planning.

10 The language is produced spontaneously.

11 Words and ideas are often repeated.

12 The language is highly organised and develops logically and sequentially.

When you are ready, read the commentary on page 75.

The lack of planning time for spoken language means that speakers often try to gain a little time by adding 'erm', 'ah', 'I mean' and so on to their language. Also they may start an utterance and realise that it does not fit with what they wanted, or were able, to say and therefore they choose to start again ('I won't…it's not that I don't want you to get married.'). This phenomenon is usually referred to as a 'false start'.

When analysed, spoken language can seem chaotic whereas written language tends to be organised and logically sequenced. Part of the reason for this is because most writing has already been corrected and re-drafted before it is read. The reader only usually sees the 'tidied up' version, whereas this is not possible when dealing with speech. The listener witnesses all the 're-drafting' as it happens in real time.

Characteristics of effective writers

We will now move on to look at how effective writers tend to operate in their own language.

Imagine that you have been on a holiday which you didn't enjoy. You believe that the information in the brochure was not accurate so you write and complain. Imagine writing to a friend about the same experience. Would the two letters be the same? If not, in what ways would they be different?

When you are ready, read the commentary on page 75.

One characteristic of an effective writer is that they will have a command of a range of styles and be able to adopt an appropriate tone. Being able to do this depends on a knowledge of the **audience**. In other words, people know who they are writing to, (or at least an understanding of the role and function of that person) and therefore can judge the appropriate tone to adopt. They will also understand and be able to use the conventions of writing (the layout expected, for example).

Now imagine writing a 2,000-word essay on teaching English. Look at the list of strategies and stages below. Tick the ones you would find useful.

- ☐ Read books and make notes
- ☐ Write a brief essay plan
- ☐ Write the essay
- ☐ Read the essay and make changes
- ☐ Check grammar and spelling

It is probable that you ticked all the stages. Typically effective writers collect information (represented above by reading books) and consider what they want to include. They organise their ideas (plan) and then write a draft of the essay, sometimes quite quickly, knowing that they will return to it and be able to revise it. They also check spelling, grammar and so on.

We can see that there is a process that effective writers go through, and that writing is not a single act but a collection of acts. It should be noted that the stages listed above may not always be followed sequentially, with one stage completed before the next happens. They may happen in parallel. For example, a writer may redraft part of an essay before the whole of the first draft is completed.

It is also expected that good writers will be able to control grammar, spelling, linking devices and so on effectively.

Having looked briefly at what good writers do in general, we will now go on to consider how these skills can be developed in the classroom. But first we will briefly consider how writing can benefit the learning process.

Writing in the classroom

Writing as an aid to learning

Some learners have no need to write in a foreign language. They may be learning English simply to go on holiday in an English-speaking country, for example. However, some writing practice may still be justified in the syllabus. This is because writing can help learning. Even at a simple level, learners who copy new language from the board into a notebook are more likely to remember it than those who don't. Although we mentioned in the chapters on teaching grammar that oral practice was very important, some written practice of new language may be useful. We tend to expect greater accuracy in writing than in speech, and so writing can be useful for helping learners to work on accuracy. We also noted that writing allows more thinking time and space for reflection than speech, and this too can sometimes be useful. In addition, short writing activities can also provide a variety of pace in a lesson and most learners expect a proportion of their lesson or lessons to include such writing activities.

Writing to communicate

When we were looking at the characteristics of effective writers, we noted that writing involves going through a process before arriving at a finished product. Look at the following comments by teachers. What aspects of the process of writing is each focusing on?

Judith: The students did a short piece of writing. Before they gave it to me I told them they had to check that they had agreements between subjects and verbs correct ('everybody like**s**') and also that infinitives (without 'to') followed any modal verb they had used.

Jon: I wanted the students to write about environmental problems, so we started by discussing the problems and what could be done about them.

Alison: I wanted the learners to do some writing practice so we started by reading a letter and they had to respond to the letter.

Kevin: The students wrote a description of someone they admired in class, but I didn't give them much time. They then had to copy it out for homework and they will give it to me tomorrow.

When you are ready, read the commentary on page 75.

Classroom activities

Some learners may need to develop writing skills to quite a high level. For example, they may wish to study at a university in an English-speaking country. Other learners, who don't need to write in English in real life, sometimes resent classroom time being spent on developing writing skills. Teachers should always be aware of learners' needs although, as we have seen, some writing practice may contribute to overall language development. We will now look at some classroom activities. For each activity, consider whether it practises writing as a means of communication, or whether writing is being used as an aid to learning.

Activity 1

Learners are given five sentences each containing the second conditional. However, the words for each sentence are jumbled up and the learners have to put them into the correct order. Example: car/really/would/if/I/million/expensive/a/had/pounds/a/I/buy

Activity 2

The learners search on the internet for an organisation they are interested in (for example, their favourite English football club). They then write either an e-mail or letter requesting to be sent information about the organisation – in the case of a football club, they may request a fixture list or a catalogue of merchandising, for example.

Activity 3

The learners work in groups of 3 to write an essay about censorship. They write on large pieces of paper, which are later displayed around the room. The learners then circulate, reading each other's work, and are invited to write comments on the essays – noting the bits they agree or disagree with. They can also highlight any bits of language that they think may be wrong (grammar mistakes, spelling problems and so on).

Activity 4

The learners are given the beginnings and endings of sentences and also a list of linking words. They must match each section to make sentences. Example:

Do you want to drive	as long as	working really hard.
She failed the exam	and then	he was never rich.
I'll lend you the money	but	went to a bar.
Tony worked hard all his life	despite	shall we go by train?
We played golf	or	you don't tell Rachel.

Activity 5
Learners write a short dialogue in pairs and then perform it for the class.

Activity 6
The teacher plays a piece of music. The learners listen to the music and imagine an empty room with a person listening to it. The teacher may prompt this with questions about physical appearance, age, job, interests and so on. The learners then listen to a second piece of music which is very different to the first and repeat the activity, again making notes. After listening, each learner chooses one set of notes and writes a paragraph or two describing the person. When they have finished they pass this to a partner who has to guess which piece of music the description goes with. At the end, the teacher collects the writing to read and correct.

Activity 7
The teacher gives out an opening paragraph of a story and all the students read it. The teacher then supplies one half of the class with one version of the ending and the other half with an alternative ending. For example, the opening paragraph could be about a whirlwind romance. One ending could be happy, the other sad. The learners work in groups to write a paragraph or two to link the common beginning and their version of the ending. The teacher then pairs students who have different endings and they read their stories to each other. At the end, the teacher collects the writing to read and correct.

Activity 8
The teacher gives the learners the following scenario: a man and a woman met for the first time last night and they are mad about each other. It's 10.20 the next morning and the woman decides to text the man. The learners are split into two groups and each group takes the part of the man or the woman. They discuss what to say and then text their message across the room. The other group discusses it and how to respond. Each group has three or four turns. The exchange is then recreated on the board. The teacher could draw attention to particular features of text messages, such as 'cu' for 'see you' and so on.

Activity 9
Learners work in pairs, using one piece of paper. They are told to have a conversation but they must not speak. Everything is to be written down. When they have finished their 'conversation' the teacher collects the writing to read and correct.

Activity 10
The teacher asks the students some standard comprehension type questions, such as: Why did John leave home? Where did he go? Who did he meet? What did he start doing? How did he become so successful? The learners must produce a text that answers these questions. They work in groups, first discussing what their story might include, and then writing the story. The teacher then puts the stories on the wall for others to read.

When you are ready, read the commentary on page 75.

Developing literacy
As we said when discussing reading, most learners have learned to read and write in their own language before they start to learn English. However, occasionally this is not the case and teachers have to teach the very basics of writing skills. Learners who have learned to read and write in their own language but whose language uses a different script, such as Arabic or Chinese, may benefit from similar activities.

Here are three activities which may help at very low levels:

1 The teacher gives each learner a piece of paper with a word written on in thick black pen. The teacher may want to use arrows to show the direction the pen should move in to form the letters and a dot to indicate the starting point. The learners place a piece of paper over the word and trace the word showing through their paper.

2 The teacher gives each learner a picture, for example of an animal. There are also cards and each card has one letter of the word written on it. The learners must place the cards in the correct order to form the word.

3 The teacher gives the learners each a set of cards. On each card is a single word. The learners must arrange the words in order to make simple sentences.

Summary

- Like speaking, writing is a means of communicating.
- Speech and writing are different in many ways.
- Effective writers tend to go through a process of writing.
- Teachers need to help learners go through a similar process.
- Writing is also a useful aid to learning.

CHAPTER

10 Commentary

Differences between writing and speech

3 S **4** S **5** W **6** W **7** S **8** S **9** W **10** S
11 S **12** W

Characteristics of effective writers

The letters would almost certainly not be the same. The letter of complaint would have a fairly formal style, whereas the letter to a friend would be more informal. There are many differences between very formal and very informal language and here are just one or two examples. Formal writing may be characterised by the use of few contractions ('do not' rather than 'don't', for example), the use of more formal vocabulary ('however', 'moreover', 'nevertheless' when linking sentences, for example). Informal language may use simpler linking devices ('and', 'but') and use contractions. The layout of the letters would probably be different (the way the reader is addressed, the closing of the letter, where, and if, addresses are included etc).

Writing in the classroom

Writing to communicate

Judith is getting the students to check their work and is giving them specific instructions on how to do it. It can be very useful to build up a 'checklist' for individual learners to ensure that when they edit their work they are looking out for their typical mistakes.
Jon is helping the learners to gather some ideas before they commit pen to paper.
Alison is using some input data. This can be very useful because it creates an audience for the learners – they know who their letter must go to. This will help learners to adopt an appropriate style in their own writing because it creates a context.
Kevin is helping learners to draft and then re-draft their work. The first draft could be seen as developing 'fluency' and the second draft focuses more on 'accuracy'. (See Chapter 12.)

Classroom activities

Activity 1 – this focuses on developing language accuracy rather than communication. Notice that it may help learners with the form of what they write (word order and so on) but it does not practise what meaning the form conveys. The correct sentence should read: *If I had a million pounds I would buy a really expensive car* or *I would buy ... if I had ...* .

Activity 2 – this is writing to communicate. It can be very motivating for learners when they receive a reply and they realise that their English was effective.

Activity 3 – this is largely communicative – the displaying of the work generates some kind of audience and the activity would lead naturally to a re-draft stage using the comments of peers. The writing is done in groups and this not only generates some communication during the writing phase but also allows students to learn from each other. Working in groups can be particularly useful for generating ideas.

Activity 4 – this focuses on the use of linking words.

Activity 5 – there may be a mixture of form and communication focus here, depending on how the teacher sets up the activity. Note that learners are unlikely to ever have to write dialogues in real life, but it provides some useful language practice.

Activity 6 – this activity involves some communication, particularly as there is a purpose to writing the description in that someone will read and match it to the appropriate piece of music. It also practises a particular set of language – that used to describe people.

Activity 7 – as above, there is an audience created for the writing and there is therefore some communication. The teacher could direct learners to a particular set of language, such as past verb forms.

Activity 8 – this is largely communicative, although there is a reflection stage built in at the end for learners to reflect on the language they have used, and this could be more form focused.

Activity 9 – clearly this involves communication. The teacher could extend the activity by asking the students to read out the conversation, but this should be included in the instructions before the learners write, because they may include things in what they assume is a private conversation that they would not want to talk to the class about.

Activity 10 – again this involves communication. The activity could be used before a reading text which also answers the questions used by the teacher. It may be motivating for learners to compare their response to that of the text.

CHAPTER

11 Developing speaking skills

In the preceding chapters we have looked at teaching the receptive skills of reading and listening and also at teaching writing skills. In that chapter we noticed some of the differences between speech and writing, including the fact that speech is often spontaneously produced in a very limited time frame. We will now look at speaking skills in a little more detail.

Do you need to teach speaking skills?

Speaking has already been discussed in this book in several places. When we looked at grammar and vocabulary lessons we noted how important it was for learners to have oral practice. We also looked at activities that could be based on output from learners – largely spoken – and then reflected on and analysed by the learners, giving them the chance to notice new vocabulary and grammar patterns, as well as looking at the mistakes made. The starting point of this kind of activity is clearly speaking. When looking at receptive skills lessons, we noticed that frequently there are stages of those lessons that provide opportunities for learners to discuss or react to what they have heard or read.

Speaking has often been dealt with in a similar way in language teaching. It is sometimes thought of as something which is covered sufficiently by virtue of being so bound up in the teaching of everything else. Paradoxically, although many learners feel that being able to communicate effectively through speech is their main priority, when speaking is the main aim of the lesson it can sometimes lead to dissatisfaction. Some learners can't quite see the point of doing something in the classroom that they could quite easily do over a coffee, and teachers can feel a sense of guilt because they have not taught something with a clear learning outcome that can be held up as justification for the lesson.

However, experience shows that dedicated speaking skills lessons can be useful. Realistic classroom speaking activities could be seen as an opportunity for rehearsing the things learners may want to do outside the classroom, but in a safe environment, where mistakes can be learned from, rather than lead to difficulties and embarrassment. We will look at the reasons people speak and what speaking involves, to try to identify what needs to be taught in a speaking skills syllabus, and how learners can be helped to develop oral fluency, accuracy, and to incorporate increasingly sophisticated features of language into their speech. But first we will look at different types of speaking.

Why do people speak?

Think of all the times you have spoken in the last twenty four hours. In each case, try to think of the purpose behind the interaction. Why were you speaking?

Now look at these situations. What is the difference between:

1 Talking to a friend and making a speech at his/her wedding

2 Talking to a friend and talking to your boss

3 Talking to a friend and talking to the newsagent when you buy a paper

When you are ready, read the commentary on page 81.

As we can see, there are many reasons why people speak to each other. One primary use of language is to establish and maintain social relationships. We say 'hello' to people when we meet them, exchange small talk about the weather, work, sport and family relationships. As part of this social use of language we also try to entertain each other by making jokes and telling anecdotes and stories. We may also share views and opinions on a variety of subjects. When we chat to friends there is no agenda of what we should cover. Those involved in the conversation can introduce a variety of subjects.

Language is also used to share or pass on information. In these contexts there will be more of a set agenda. This need not take the form of a set of listed points to be covered in a meeting, but there will be an understanding of what should or should not be talked about. During a business presentation we would be surprised if the speaker continually introduced unrelated topics.

Some speaking is based on performing a transaction of some kind. When I phone up to order a curry to be delivered to my house, both participants work together to achieve the transaction as efficiently as possible. In this situation the language is highly predictable. The conversation follows precisely the same pattern every time.

In both social and work contexts language may also be used to discuss options and solve problems. In addition we use language to manage the interaction itself. For example, we can say when we don't understand something, or haven't heard part of what was said. We can also use language to invite others to speak, ('What do you think, Debbie?'), and so language is used to ensure that the interaction proceeds smoothly.

So, people speak to maintain existing social relationships and to make new ones. They also speak to pool and exchange information and also to ease the performance of transactions. These categories are broad and could be subdivided further, but they cover some of the main reasons people speak.

What does speaking involve?

Speaking involves many different things. We have already seen that the spoken language used in some contexts may be highly predictable, (for example, when ordering a meal to be delivered) in others it may be unpredictable. In some contexts people may speak for a short time and other people may rapidly 'take the floor', with turns being taken very quickly. This happens in most social conversation. At other times people may have to speak for an extended time.

Look at the following questions and try to answer them.

1 In what ways may casual conversation be harder to take part in for a learner than giving a presentation?

2 To what extent does speaking involve a knowledge of vocabulary and grammar?

3 When listening to someone speaking a foreign language, what other things can make it difficult for the listener(s) to understand?

4 To what extent can learners correct their own mistakes as they speak?

5 Do you think that the language background and the culture of the learner may affect how they perform in English?

When you are ready, read the commentary on page 81.

So, in order to speak, and express what they want to, people must recall the appropriate words and organise them into units (grammar awareness). They must also move lips, tongue and so on to form the appropriate sounds, monitor what comes out and be prepared to correct it. In addition to all this, speakers need an awareness of cultural conventions, which may limit what it is appropriate to say, or how something is expressed. For native speakers this all happens exceptionally quickly, but typically much more slowly in a foreign language, and so in unpredictable conversational settings even fairly high level learners can find it difficult to participate effectively.

What learners need to practise and learn

Look at this summary of what learners need to be able to do in order to speak effectively in a variety of situations. Remember, speaking often happens under very strict time pressure.

1 Learners need to carry out 'routine' exchanges – for example, when greeting someone or buying a newspaper.

2 Learners need to take part in unpredictable exchanges – for example, casual conversation.

3 Learners need to know when it is appropriate to speak, how they can politely interrupt and so on.

4 Learners need to monitor what they say, so that they can correct it if necessary.

5 Learners need to be able to 'negotiate' and manage exchanges – inviting others to speak, asking for repetition, and so on.

6 Learners need to speak with intelligible pronunciation.

7 Learners need to select appropriate vocabulary and use grammar to organise what they say.

As we have seen in earlier chapters, separate grammar and vocabulary activities, assuming they provide a lot of oral practice, should help with the last point. We looked at ways in which learners can be helped with pronunciation in Chapter 7. We will now focus on the first five points in the list. Look at the classroom activities described below. Match the activities (A–E) with numbers 1–5.

A

The teacher teaches the expressions: 'So, do you mean that…?', 'I didn't understand the last thing you said', and 'Could you speak a little slower, please?'.

B

The learners work in groups of four. Three of the students are given different questions written on a piece of paper (such as 'What did you do last night?). None of the students are told what the others will ask. The fourth student must answer their questions and try to ask a question in return on the same topic. The group must try to ask and answer all the questions, with no pause lasting for more than two seconds.

Student A: What did you do last night?
Student B: I watched a video. And you?
Student A: Nothing much.
Student C: Where are you from?
Student A: Chile. Have you been there? *etc.*

C

The teacher gives the class a typical error that is being made. For example, *these* + singular noun ('these idea'). During a speaking activity, every time a speaker makes that particular error she must correct it before another student can say the correct form.

D

The teacher elicits a dialogue between a shopkeeper and a customer, with the learners practising it line by line. Learners then perform the role play with partners.

E

The teacher teaches expressions such as: 'I'm sorry, I didn't mean to interrupt you', and 'Sorry, you go first'.

When you are ready, check your answer on page 81.

Considerations when conducting speaking lessons

We will now move on to look at some of the practicalities involved when conducting speaking lessons. Look at the statements below and decide if you agree or disagree with them. You could base your decisions on any experience you have had as a language learner, or on what you have read so far in this book.

1 All speaking lessons should be conducted in open class situations – with the teacher addressing the whole class or one student addressing the class.

2 Pair and group work will only lead to students learning the mistakes of their colleagues.

3 All mistakes should be corrected.

4 What the learners say is not important – it is only important that they speak English accurately.

5 As soon as the learners start talking about something other than the given task, the teacher should ensure that the learners refocus on what they should be doing.

6 All learners must speak for approximately the same length of time in all lessons.

When you are ready, check your answers on page 82.

Example speaking activities

Read the descriptions of classroom activities and answer the questions that follow.

Classroom activity 1

This is a problem-solving activity. It is a survival game in which learners must work together to develop a survival strategy. They imagine that the light aircraft they have been travelling in has been forced to make an emergency landing. There are items in the plane that they can take and they must put them in order of usefulness. The items include such things as water, a box of matches, a gun and so on. The learners think for a couple of minutes about what they think is important and then work in groups to discuss their strategy and the potential value of each item. The teacher monitors the activity and later invites each group to report on their decisions, and then corrects some of the language mistakes that she heard.

1 Look back at the list of 7 points under 'What learners need to practise and learn'. Which of the points may be practised in this activity?

Classroom activity 2

The teacher dictates the beginning of eight sentences. The learners must write what she says and complete the sentences for themselves. For example: 'In the future I hope to…; My perfect job would be…'
(and other examples).

A learner writes:
In the future I hope to *travel around the world.* (and completes the other sentence stems appropriately).

The teacher then puts the learners into groups to discuss the ways in which they have completed the sentences and to ask each other questions about what they have written: '*What countries would you like to go to?*' and so on. The teacher listens to the discussion and later corrects.

2 What skills, as well as speaking, are practised here?

3 Could this activity be used with different level classes?

Classroom activity 3

The teacher sets up the following role play. There is a proposal to build a new chemical factory in a town. Some residents think this is a good idea because there is currently high unemployment. Some residents think this is a bad idea because they are concerned about the risks of pollution. Each student is given a card with their role described. For example, there are two representatives from the company, concerned parents, a doctor, unemployed workers and so on. The students are given time to prepare what they want to say and then they perform the role play. The teacher listens and only becomes involved if communication breaks down. She later corrects.

4 What are the advantages of using a role play?

5 What are the disadvantages?

Classroom activity 4

There are sixteen learners in a class. The teacher organises the room so that there are two concentric circles. The learners sit facing each other. The teacher writes three topics on the board (such as 'Blood sports should be banned', 'Why I love my country', and 'Tourism is nearly always a bad thing'). The learners work in pairs (with the person they are facing) and must choose one of the topics, which they then discuss for three minutes. The teacher then stops the activity and writes two or three more topics on the board. All the learners in the outer circle move around one place and with their new partner decide on which topic they want to talk about and again they have three minutes in which to do so. The activity continues until all the students in the outer circle have spoken to all the learners in the inner circle. The teacher then conducts a feedback session, including some correction of mistakes.

6 Does this activity practise accuracy or fluency? (See page 83)

7 What are the advantages and disadvantages of the amount of movement?

Classroom activity 5

Learners work in pairs, A and B. The teacher places several copies of a short text (say, 10-15 lines) around the room. Student A must run to a copy of the text, remember a chunk and then run back to her partner and dictate what she remembers. She must then run back to the text, remember and dictate again. This continues until she has successfully dictated the complete text. The first pair to finish wins. As pairs finish, so the teacher gives them a copy of the text and they check that their version is the same as the original.

8 As well as speaking, what skills are practised?

When you are ready, read the commentary on page 82.

Notice that in the first three activities described the learners have a few moments at least to think about the language they will need to use. Research shows that planning time often leads to more accurate language production and, importantly, to learners being more ambitious with the language forms they attempt to use. Also each activity is followed by some reflection on the language generated, perhaps in the form of error correction, but the teacher can also feed in useful bits of new language or highlight examples of good language use.

Speaking is a very important skill for nearly all learners. Some, however, feel shy and embarrassed when called on to speak, and others, while being fairly fluent, make so many errors that understanding their meaning can be difficult. Speaking lessons allow learners to practise their existing skills in a protected and safe environment. This can increase their confidence, and therefore boost their performance when they have to speak in a real world situation. By supplying new bits of language and using correction techniques effectively, the teacher can help learners to perform better than they could without support. Again, this improvement may transfer to situations outside the classroom. Lessons, or parts of lessons, which are designed to improve oral fluency and accuracy should be part of most syllabuses.

Summary

- Most learners feel that developing speaking skills is essential.
- Not all the skills necessary for speaking effectively will necessarily be covered in other lessons.
- The classroom provides an ideal, 'protected' environment in which learners can develop confidence in speaking English.
- Teachers need to provide a variety of speaking activities to reflect the variety of speaking activities learners will engage in in real life.

CHAPTER

11 Commentary

Why do people speak?

1 ***Talking to a friend and making a speech at his/her wedding***
A speech will be characterised by a long turn (a speaker speaking without interruption), whereas when we talk to friends there will be short turns, where people say a few words and then someone else contributes, and so on. The content of a wedding speech will be dictated partly by tradition – there are things the audience expects to hear – but when speaking to a friend there will be no particular agenda. People will speak about whatever seems important or interesting at the time.

2 ***Talking to a friend and talking to your boss***
It is likely that different topics will be discussed in these situations. In a work context there is likely to be a set topic and issues outside those related to work may not be acceptable. The formality of the language will also vary because the power relationship between friends is equal, but this is not the case when speaking to a boss. This may affect who initiates conversational exchanges – typically the person with more power or authority – and also the choice of vocabulary used.

3 ***Talking to a friend and talking to the newsagent when you buy a paper***
The discussion with the newsagent may be 'transactional' in nature. S/he asks for a certain amount of money, you give it, say thank you, and leave. There is unlikely to be any development beyond what is essential for the transaction to be completed. This is obviously different to speaking to a friend, where there is no transaction as such, and the purpose is to build or maintain social relationships.

What does speaking involve?

1 Although the presentation calls for an extended period of speaking, at least the learner will have time to prepare and to practise what they want to say, unlike in conversations. They could use grammar reference books and dictionaries, as well as practising pronunciation of particular words or phrases beforehand. In a presentation the learner will also be able to focus totally on speaking, whereas conversation involves listening and decoding what others are saying, and having to respond very quickly.

2 Learners need to know enough vocabulary to express what they want and also to organise it in a way which the listeners can understand. Therefore vocabulary and grammar are essential.

3 Poor pronunciation (see Chapter 7) may make listening difficult.

4 They may be able to correct themselves to some extent, but if they pay a lot of attention to accuracy they may lose fluency (speaking without too many pauses and hesitations – see Chapter 12) and listeners may become frustrated. Native speakers frequently pause and correct what they say.

5 Culture will play an important part in speaking. The strategies we use for interrupting others, showing disapproval, inviting others to speak, and knowing how long it is appropriate to speak for may vary in different cultures. Therefore learners may not be able to transfer appropriately their awareness of their own language to the speaking of another.

What learners need to practise and learn

1 D **2** B **3** E **4** C **5** A

Activity A gives learners formulaic language to help them manage conversations.
Activity B tries to replicate some of the unpredictability of much spoken language and tries to add an element of time pressure, which is typical of spoken language.
Activity C tries to encourage learners to monitor the language they produce.
Activity D helps learners to take part in predictable exchanges. Often such exchanges can be taught at quite a low level.
Activity E tries to give learners fixed expressions to use if they mistime their contribution to a conversation, and so helps them to become more confident when interrupting others.

Considerations when conducting speaking lessons

1 This is not the case, other than when groups are very small. Parts of lessons may be conducted in this way – typically the feedback stages – but learners will simply not get enough speaking practice if only one person can speak at a time. Also it will encourage the learners to rely on being prompted to speak by the teacher, rather than practising strategies of turn taking, interrupting and other features of normal speech. Much of the time should be spent with the learners speaking to each other in pairs and groups.

2 There is little evidence supporting the idea that learners will pick up a lot of mistakes made by others and incorporate them into their own language. However, it is something that learners worry about, and so they need to be reassured that the teacher is listening to what they say, and will pick up on mistakes later in the lesson. Monitoring pairs and groups is very important.

3 This is not necessarily the case. Mistakes that interfere with meaning need to be addressed, but speaking effectively demands a degree of confidence, and too much correction can destroy this. Teachers need to be sensitive in their approach and to treat learners as individuals. Some learners may benefit from a lot of correction while others may need very little.

4 Both aspects are important – what they say and how they say it. The teacher should get feedback from learners on what they said (this is important because it demonstrates the value of communication and that language is about more than the manipulation of certain forms), and also give feedback on how it was said. (See Chapter 13)

5 Many teachers would agree with this, although it should be remembered that in most conversations the topic does change rapidly and therefore occasionally this may be quite useful practice, assuming that it is done in English.

6 This is not necessarily true. Certainly all learners should be given the opportunity to speak but some may be naturally more inclined to listen than perform, and may still benefit from this. If learners are shy about speaking in front of the whole class then pair work and group work can be a very useful way of building confidence.

Example speaking activities

Classroom activity 1

1 This does not practise routine, predictable exchanges. It does practise taking part in an unpredictable exchange. It practises the skills of when to speak, how to interrupt and so on, and also gives learners the opportunity to try to correct mistakes as they make them. Learners have to negotiate and manage the exchange and speak with reasonable pronunciation, as well as selecting appropriate vocabulary and grammar. Notice too that the teacher ensures that learners perceive the value of the activity by correcting them afterwards, as well as supplying pieces of new language. The teacher could also choose to highlight any items of language used that focused on a particular speaking sub-skill, such as apologising for interrupting inappropriately.

Classroom activity 2

2 There is listening (in order to write down what the teacher says), writing, speaking, and more listening (in the discussion).

3 Yes, the sentence stems can be adapted to suit the interests and level of the class, making it a very flexible activity. Notice too that the learners talk about themselves. Personalisation is often considered to be beneficial to language learning.

Classroom activity 3

4 Learners who are uncomfortable discussing their personal views often enjoy role play. Teachers can select learners for roles so that mixed levels can be catered for because different roles will have different linguistic demands. We have seen that people speak differently according to the context. Therefore it can be good practice to speak to someone in role play of higher or lower status (patient/doctor, boss/employee).

5 Some learners want to express their own views and resent having to pretend to support other views. Some learners associate role play with acting and thus feel embarrassed. However, teachers can start with very short simple scenarios and build up to a more complex one, such as this.

Classroom activity 4

6 The discussion is fluency based but the correction at the end provides a focus on accuracy.

7 The movement and frequent changes of partner seem to generate a lot of energy. The teacher needs to ensure that instructions are clear – the learners in the inner circle do not move and those in the outer circle move one place at a time and always in the same direction. This demands careful management.

Classroom activity 5

8 Reading (student A), writing (student B), and listening. The movement creates a great deal of energy in the classroom and allows all four skills to be practised in a fun way.

CHAPTER

12 Fluency and accuracy

What do we mean by fluency and accuracy?

Look at the views below of two teachers. Who do you agree with more? If you have been taught a language, which approach did your teacher take, or did they combine the two?

> Andrew:
> *The most important thing is for the students to speak quite confidently. I don't care if they make a few mistakes as long as they can be understood. They just need to get their message across effectively.*
>
> Karen:
> *I hate it when my students make careless mistakes. I always encourage them to think carefully and try to avoid getting things wrong.*

Andrew's view is prioritising fluency. Fluency, in ELT, does not necessarily mean being able to speak like a native speaker, but means instead having the ability to produce reasonably large amounts of language fairly quickly – it is characterised by the ability to 'keep going' and being able to get the message across effectively without undue pauses and hesitations. It is focused on communication. Karen, on the other hand, prizes accuracy. This is the ability to produce language which is relatively free of mistakes. Typically, classroom activities which are designed to promote accuracy focus on one language point, or a small set of language points. In these activities manipulating forms and meaning appropriately is sometimes more important than communicating real opinions, emotions and feelings.

The terms fluency and accuracy are most commonly applied to speaking skills, but are occasionally also used to describe writing ability. It could be argued that the terms could also be applied to listening and reading, where fluency would equate to understanding quite large amounts of text quite quickly (a gist-type understanding) and accuracy would equate to a slower, more detailed, understanding.

The discussion here will be based primarily on speaking. There is clearly an overlap with lessons that present new vocabulary or new grammar because in these lessons the learners also need to practise the new language, and this will involve speaking (or other skills). Some practice activities will focus on fluency and others on accuracy.

What is the relationship between fluency and accuracy?

1 What problems might a learner encounter who focused largely on fluency?

2 What problems might a learner encounter who focused largely on accuracy?

When you are ready, read the commentary on page 87.

It is clear that learners need a balance between developing fluency and accuracy. Fluency which is achieved at the expense of any attention to accuracy may become incomprehensible and communicatively worthless. It is reasonable to assume that fluency and accuracy will impact upon one another. If a learner consciously tries to avoid mistakes (i.e. be more accurate) they are likely to do so at the expense of fluency. They will, for example, probably need to hesitate more as they think of the next thing to say. Similarly, if a learner attempts to 'keep going' and communicate reasonably freely, they may well make more mistakes.

Different methods and approaches in language teaching make different assumptions about the relationship between fluency and accuracy. Many traditional approaches assume that accuracy should be prioritised and when learners have learned how to be accurate, so they can become more fluent. In the classroom this often reveals itself in the ordering of practice activities. Having presented a new language point of vocabulary or grammar the teacher will proceed through relatively controlled practice (with a high degree of accuracy expected) to 'freer' practice, which will help to develop fluency.

However, this accuracy to fluency model is not used exclusively, and many researchers feel that developing an ability to communicate is more likely to lead to accuracy than the other way round. Therefore, in some approaches, such as task based learning, the initial focus will be on communication, and then there may be a period of reflection which focuses on accuracy.

A common technique used in many classrooms is to set the learners an activity in pairs or groups so that they communicate reasonably naturally. For example, the learners may discuss the value of television in small groups. After this discussion there is a 'reporting back' stage, where a spokesperson for the group tells the class what the group talked about. It could be argued that this format naturally includes a demand for both fluency and accuracy. As learners discuss ideas with their class colleagues, the primary focus for most students will be on fluency. It is a semi-private, relatively informal discussion. However, when reporting back, the student nominated has to speak in front of the entire class, including the teacher, and this context is likely to lead the student to want to avoid errors, and therefore focus on accuracy.

Notice how in this example the need for accuracy develops naturally from the context in which the learners are asked to perform.

Teachers may choose to plan lessons which move from an accuracy focus to fluency, or vice versa. The important thing is that learners engage in activities which give them the opportunity to develop in both areas, and variety is in itself a good thing. Teachers should not feel that every lesson must start with accuracy and progress towards fluency, or indeed that fluency must always precede accuracy. When teaching vocabulary or grammar it is necessary to provide a balance of activities which help to develop both fluency and accuracy.

The teacher clearly has some control over whether the learners focus on fluency or accuracy by choosing the activities the class engages in. However, learners also come with their own ideas of what is important when learning a language. This is sometimes shaped by their previous learning experience or what they feel their needs are. Some learners will naturally prize being able to speak fluently, despite making mistakes, and others will value avoiding errors.

It is probably the case that the best learners pay attention to both of these facets of communication and therefore the teacher needs to encourage those learners who naturally strive for fluency to pay some attention to accuracy, and vice versa.

Ways of developing fluency and accuracy

We have so far discussed the need for teachers to plan lessons so that learners develop both fluency and accuracy. The priority the teacher gives to each may depend on the needs of the learners, their existing strengths and weaknesses, as well as the level at which they are studying. We will now look at some specific examples of activities that could be used.

Of course, when called upon to speak, some learners may prioritise fluency while others may prioritise accuracy. We can therefore only really say that the activities have the **potential** to develop fluency or accuracy.

Look at the brief descriptions of activities below.

1 Decide if you think that the primary focus is on fluency, accuracy or a combination of the two.

2 Read the commentary on page 87.

3 Write the name of each activity.

4 Give each activity a 'star rating':
3 = really good
2 = OK
1 = I don't like the sound of this activity

Activity 1:
Star rating:

The teacher sets up a situation with two characters and a situation. For example, a patient and a doctor are discussing the patient's health problem. The teacher elicits what each character would say, line by line, and writes it on the board. The learners are divided into pairs, and practise and perform the dialogue with a partner.

Activity 2:
Star rating:

The teacher organises a discussion, either in small groups or in open class. For example, learners discuss whether they agree that blood sports should be banned.

Activity 3:
Star rating:

The teacher says a new piece of language. The class listens and then repeats.

Activity 4:
Star rating:

The learners work in pairs and are given a few minutes to prepare a story about a given situation or on a particular topic. Later one of them then tells the story to the rest of the class.

Activity 5:
Star rating:

The learners are asked to prepare a short presentation on something they are interested in (perhaps as part of their homework). In a future lesson the learners give their presentations.

Activity 6:
Star rating:

The learners are given a problem to solve. The information required to solve the problem is shared between members of the class and they therefore have to work together to find the solution. For example, a crime is described and each member of the class has a different clue, which when put together with the others will lead to the discovery of who committed it.

Activity 7:
Star rating:

The class is divided into teams. Each learner is given a different topic and must try to speak for 60 seconds on that topic, without excessive hesitation. If they are successful they score a point for their team. If they only manage to speak for a part of the time, a member of the other team has to speak for the remainder of the time to score a point.

Activity 8:
Star rating:

Each member of the class is given a role. For example, a company is planning to make redundancies and is willing to pay a small amount of compensation. Two learners take the parts of directors, another represents the view of the trade union, which argues for greater investment by the company, another learner takes the part of a worker who would like to leave, and another a worker who is scared of losing his/her job. The learners act out their parts in groups.

Activity 9:
Star rating:

The teacher has been teaching comparative adjectives (*bigger*, *smaller*, *more interesting* etc.). She says the words 'The Nile' and 'The Thames' and the learners have to produce a sentence (e.g. 'The Nile is longer than the Thames'), and this is repeated with similar pairs of prompts.

Activity 10:
Star rating:

Learners are put into pairs. Student A has different information to Student B. They must not show their information to each other but must ask questions and talk to each other to find out the missing information.

Student A	**Student B**
Name: Rebecca Mills	Name: Rebecca Mills
Age: 34	Age:
Job:	Job: Lawyer
Marital status: Married	Marital status:
Children:	Children: 2, Jessica (4) and Sonia (2)
Telephone number: 07761 171678	Telephone number:
Salary:	Salary: £91,000
Favourite food: Curry	Favourite food:
Car:	Car: Mercedes

For example:

Student B: *How old is she?*

Student A: *34. What does she do?*

Having read the commentary, you will realise that the above activities have different strengths and weaknesses. All are potentially useful, although they may not all be useful in all situations. For example, a low level class could not be expected to take part in a discussion (Activity 2) and higher level learners may not need to listen and repeat (Activity 3) very often. When choosing activities it is essential to consider what will be useful to your particular learners.

Summary

- Learners need to develop both fluency and accuracy.
- Teachers need to provide a balance of activity types so that this can be achieved.
- Fluency and accuracy are related, but it is not clear if one leads naturally to the other in classroom learning situations.

CHAPTER

12 Commentary

What is the relationship between fluency and accuracy?

1 A learner who focused only on fluency may make numerous mistakes. This could make the communication difficult to understand and therefore place an unreasonable burden on the listener. Even if the message is clear, if no attention is paid to accuracy, the learner may retain many features of low level English despite studying for some time, persistently making elementary mistakes.

2 A learner who focuses only on accuracy may find it difficult to take part in communication outside the classroom, because they need too long to prepare each piece of language. This may place an unreasonable burden on the listener.

Ways of developing fluency and accuracy

Activity 1: Dialogue building
A useful and flexible activity at most levels. This can be used to combine fluency and accuracy – the teacher elicits language from the learners which may involve them communicating fluently, and the teacher helps them to tidy the language up (make it more accurate), before putting it on the board and practising it further.

Activity 2: Discussion
Usually an enjoyable lesson as long as you have a class that are willing to voice opinions. Clearly fluency is catered for, and so the teacher needs to build in an accuracy stage (perhaps by correcting some mistakes – see the following chapter), to extend it to its full potential. Not usually appropriate for low level learners, and learners from some cultures may be reticent about voicing personal opinions.

Activity 3: Listen and repeat
Learners often enjoy this, particularly at low levels. The value may depend on what exactly the students are repeating. Useful to help develop accurate pronunciation and to build confidence. It could be argued that the pieces of language that are repeated become more automatic for the students – needing less thought – and therefore this activity may also help to develop fluency. This is particularly true of set phrases and chunks of language.

Activity 4: Story telling
Usually a useful and enjoyable activity. Fluency is clearly prioritised, so again the teacher needs to create an accuracy focus after the activity, by focusing on some of the mistakes made, or highlighting good examples of language usage.

Activity 5: Presentations
Usually quite a popular activity. Some learners prepare very thoroughly and tend to avoid mistakes, sometimes by using notes. Others develop fluency by talking with less preparation.

Activity 6: Problem solving
The focus is on communication and the outcome of solving the problem. Fluency is favoured, so again some reflection and accuracy work can be useful afterwards.

Activity 7: Just a minute
Enjoyable, if not very realistic practice. Fluency prioritised.

Activity 8: Role play
Potentially quite a useful activity. Some students enjoy playing a role and not talking about their own opinions and feelings, others respond less well. Fluency is prioritised and the teacher could usefully build in an accuracy focus after the activity.

Activity 9: Drill
Learners often like this kind of practice. Accuracy is prioritised and there is no really genuine communication. However, drills can often be adapted to make them more communicative. For example, learners could be given a prompt such as 'tall' and respond with a true fact about their family, e.g. *'My brother is taller than me'.*

Activity 10: Information gaps
A useful activity because some communication takes place although the amount of language required is limited and can therefore focus on a particular language point. In this case the communicative value is weakened because Rebecca Mills is not a real person and therefore it is unlikely that the learners will have any genuine interest in her. However, the activity could be made more relevant and motivating by replacing Rebecca with a real person such as David Beckham, or something else of interest such as cities, countries, or historic sites.

CHAPTER

13 Correcting learners

A note on terminology:

Although in most contexts we would probably see 'error' and 'mistake' as being more or less interchangeable, in ELT a distinction is often drawn.

A mistake has been used to mean that although the learner produces an 'incorrect' utterance, or written mistake, they actually know the correct form – they simply got it wrong on that occasion, perhaps they weren't concentrating, or perhaps trying to speak, or write, too fast. It can be assumed that with a prompt from the teacher they would be able to correct themselves. However, we will use 'slip' to refer to this, clearly distinguishing it from an error.

An error is used to mean that the learner produces an 'incorrect' utterance and would be unable to correct themselves. They don't know how to use the piece of language correctly. An error is, therefore, by definition, systematic and, in theory, no amount of prompting from the teacher would help the learner correct the error because they don't know how to do so.

'Mistake' will be used as umbrella term covering both concepts – a slip and an error. This will be useful as it is often unclear which of the two categories an incorrect utterance, or written mistake, falls into.

Approaches to mistakes

Teachers sometimes have varying attitudes to correction and we will start by looking at some of these. The discussion is based on spoken language and there is a separate section which deals with written mistakes.

Look at the three remarks made by teachers. Which ones do you think are/would be closest to your feelings?

Rebecca: *I hate it when my learners make mistakes. I don't want them to learn bad habits.*

Helen: *Correcting learners seems a bit of a waste of time – they only make the same mistakes the next time.*

David: *I try to differentiate between slips and errors. I try to help learners when they make errors but ignore it if I think it is just a slip.*

Sophie: *I love it when learners make mistakes. I really feel I can teach them something that will help.*

When you are ready, read the commentary on page 93.

Of course, learners also bring with them attitudes about correction and it is worth the teacher asking them about these views at, or near, the start of the course. Most learners tend to see correction as an important part of learning and expect the teacher to correct their mistakes.

When to correct

Put a tick next to the comments you identify with. If you have no teaching experience you will not be able to respond to the third and fifth statements.

- ☐ I think I should correct every mistake.
- ☐ I try to correct most errors but I don't think it is important to correct slips.
- ☐ I would like to correct more but I find it hard to hear all the mistakes.
- ☐ I correct more during accuracy phases of a lesson than fluency phases.
- ☐ I sometimes can't correct the learner because I can't work out what she was trying to say!
- ☐ I always try to let the learner who made the mistake correct herself before I do.
- ☐ If the learner who made the mistake can't correct herself then I ask if another student can.
- ☐ I never just say 'that's wrong' – I always try to show the student which bit of what they said was wrong.
- ☐ I often feel awkward correcting learners – it seems so wrong because I can't speak their languages at all and I don't want to embarrass them.

Try to think what has led you to tick the statements you have. Were your judgements based on your own learning experiences or more of an instinctive feeling?

When you are ready, read the commentary on page 93.

Are there any occasions when you should not correct?

Below are five reasons why a teacher may decide not to correct, either immediately or after the activity. Do you think they are all good reasons?

1 When a new student in the class speaks for the first time.

2 When a learner is communicating something which is very important to them. For example, that they have just broken up with their partner.

3 When you are doing an activity of which the main aim is to help the group relax and enjoy the following parts of the lesson.

4 The teacher is angry with the learner because they are being disruptive.

5 When you are conducting feedback on a reading or listening text, and although the learner says the correct answer s/he makes a small grammar mistake in doing so.

When you are ready, read the commentary on page 94.

Ways of correcting learners

Fluency activities

Imagine you have a class of 18 learners. You have divided them into six groups of three and they are discussing the best way to advertise a new computer game.

The teacher's role is to monitor – or to listen to what the students are saying. After the students have finished, the teacher can put some of the mistakes (or good examples of language) on the board. There is no need to identify who made the errors but the teacher can ask all the learners to look at the mistakes and try to correct them. This sounds easy – and it is – as long as you can remember what you heard! It's a good idea to make notes as you listen.

Answer the following questions.

1 Who corrects the mistakes?

2 What would the alternative be if this strategy were unsuccessful?

3 What is the advantage of delaying the correction until after the activity?

When you are ready, check your answers on page 94.

A variation on this is for the teacher to prepare a sheet of mistakes that learners have made over the lesson, or over the last few lessons. This can be photocopied and learners can work in small groups to try to correct them. Again, the learners who made the mistakes remain anonymous. When the learners have finished the task, the teacher can go through all the mistakes to ensure that they have been corrected appropriately.

Accuracy activities

You are teaching a group of elementary learners. You are teaching them how to talk about the past. One of the students says:
'Yesterday we go to the beach.'

Do you....
a) ignore the mistake.
b) say 'Yesterday we went to the beach'.
c) say 'In the past, so...'

When you are ready, check your answer on page 94.

One of the differences between correcting mistakes in fluency activities and accuracy activities is that you do not have the luxury of time – the time between hearing the mistake and drawing it to the learners' attention. However the same principles apply. It's important to **highlight where** the mistake is, or the **type** of mistake, and also to **involve the learners** in the correction process.

Teachers often use gestures to indicate the type of mistake or where it is in the utterance. In the example above, rather than saying 'in the past', a teacher may choose to 'point to the past' by pointing over their shoulder.

A small number of gestures that a class becomes used to and immediately understands can speed up the correction process.

Match the gestures with the mistakes.

1 I must to phone Cindy tomorrow.

2 It is beautiful day.

3 You can tell me the time?

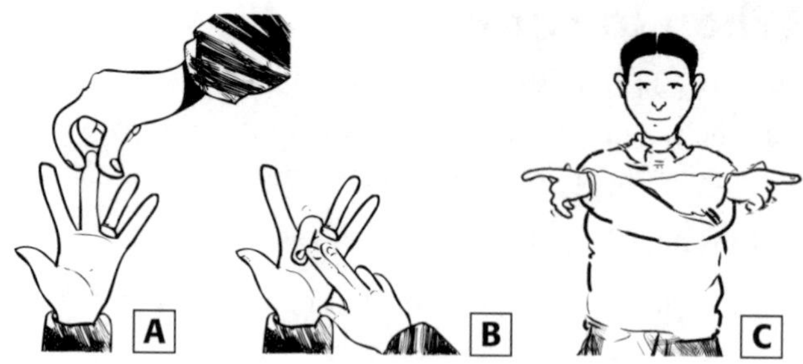

Check your answers on page 94.

Using your fingers to indicate words in a sentence is particularly useful because it so clearly highlights which bit the learners should focus on. However, for obvious reasons, this technique can only be used with fairly short stretches of text and teachers need to take care to ensure that learners 'see' the sentence going from left to right. Because learners are usually sitting in front of the teacher, this means that the teacher needs to work from right to left.

There are many other correction techniques teachers use. Look at the three described below. Mark each one in the following way:
✔ I would definitely use this idea
○ I may use this idea
✘ I do not like this idea.

1 The teacher repeats the utterance up to the mistake.
Student: It depends of you.
Teacher: It depends...
Student: It depends on you.

2 The teacher tells the learner the correct form.
Student: It depends of you.
Teacher: On you. It depends on you.

3 The teacher indicates where the error is by using a grammar term. For example,
Student: It depends of you.
Teacher: Preposition.
Student: It depends on you.

When you are ready, read the commentary on page 94.

Remember, if the mistake is actually an error rather than a slip, the learner will not be able to self correct and the teacher could invite others to participate by saying something such as 'Can anyone help?'.

Correcting pronunciation errors

One easy way to correct pronunciation is to say 'Pronunciation' (in the same way as '3' above) and hope that the student can self correct. Another way is simply to model the correct pronunciation and hope that the learner can copy it. However, s/he may not be able to and the correction process can create additional stress, making it less likely the learner will be successful. A phrase such as 'That's better – keep practising' can be very useful if the learner has already had a couple of tries. The teacher can remember that s/he needs to give more personalised help later.

If the learners already know the phonemic script (see Chapter 7), this offers a simple way of correcting the mispronunciation of individual sounds. By pointing to the appropriate symbol the teacher can help the learner to make the correct sound.

Below are some more methods of correcting pronunciation problems. Match the mistakes on the left with the correction on the right.

1 student produces 'willage' for 'village'	**A** teacher repeats the utterance, while indicating the direction of the voice by waving their arm
2 student puts the stress on the first syllable of 'photographer'	**B** teacher says 'bite your bottom lip when you say it'.
3 student uses an inappropriate intonation pattern	**C** teacher says 'de DA de de'

Check your answers on page 95.

Giving feedback on written work

Approaches

It is important to differentiate 'giving feedback on' and 'correcting' written work. Giving feedback implies that good elements of the language will be praised, as well as mistakes highlighted. Correction is part of giving feedback, but without praise and encouragement writing activities can demotivate learners. For this reason, it is better to try to avoid too many errors occurring by ensuring that the learners are sufficiently prepared to undertake the task set. This may involve brainstorming activities to gather ideas, the pre-teaching of any essential words and phrases, and ensuring that the task is not beyond the scope of the majority of learners in the group.

There are many ways of giving feedback. Perhaps the easiest is for the teacher to write comments on the paper, including what s/he assumes to be the correct versions of any mistakes. (This is not always easy because s/he may not know what the learner intended to say.) We should also remember some of the principles of error correction that we have identified earlier in the chapter. These included:

- It is a good idea to involve learners in the correction process and see if they can correct their own mistakes.
- It is a good idea to tell the learner the type of mistake made.
- It is a good idea to indicate the position of the mistake.

As we can see, if the teacher simply supplies the correct version the learner does not have the chance to be involved in the correction process and is therefore less likely to learn from it. The challenge is to find a way of involving learners even when they may not be physically present when the teacher reads the text. One way of achieving this is to use a system of symbols which indicate the position and nature of the mistakes. The teacher then returns the work, the learner corrects it and resubmits. The teacher then checks that the correction has been done successfully.

The following is a simple 'code' which could be adopted by teachers.

WW = wrong word
WO = wrong word order
Sp = spelling
G = grammar
T = Tense
P = Punctuation
un = unnecessary word
+ = add a word, or part of a word

This code is a rough guide for learners. Mistakes are notoriously difficult to classify and the categories overlap. All tense mistakes are grammar mistakes, and some grammar mistakes could be classified as being the result of a wrong word choice, or even a spelling mistake. However, the code is likely to give sufficient guidance for learners to to re-draft their work and therefore to benefit.

Example

Look at the following piece of writing. Intermediate level learners were asked to write a letter to a British Council office asking for information about English language exams. All of the mistakes were made by the class, although they have been edited together here to form one text. Correct the writing using the symbols above and then compare your corrections with those in the commentary on page 95.

> *Dear Sir/Madam*
>
> *I am writting to ask for some informations.*
> *My English is not perfect but I am studing English for several years in a large langauge school at Santiago, Chile. I want take a exam in the nearest future. I do not do any English exams before. If possible I would like to have IELTS exam. I would like to know how many parts does the exam consist of? Should I registrate in advance? How much is it costs? I am also interesting in some practice material. Can you give me any advices. Please send me all necessary detail. Thank you for your help. I look forward to hear from you.*
>
> *Yours sincerely*
>
> *Alejandra Gomez*

Many teachers find this technique useful. However, one drawback with it is that it is very time consuming because the work is handed in once, marked, handed back and then has to be re-marked. An alternative approach, which still involves learners in the correction of mistakes, is for the teacher to write out some of the mistakes made and photocopy it for learners to correct in small groups.

For more controlled activities, where written answers are more predictable, the teacher can involve learners by giving them answer sheets when they complete an activity and asking them to look for their own mistakes. For example, if a teacher uses a dictation activity, s/he can then give a 'correct' version to the learners and ask them to look for differences. Either before this, or as an alternative to it, learners could be asked to compare their answers with a partner's version of the same activity. Seeing differences between the two versions may lead to learners seeing and correcting mistakes.

Summary

- Correct a lot – learners generally expect it and want to be corrected.
- Correct clearly and briefly.
- Involve learners in correction work through self and peer correction – avoid simply telling them the correct version all the time.
- You do not always have to correct immediately. Delayed correction can also be useful.
- Mistakes that involve a breakdown in communication **do** need to be dealt with immediately, whatever stage of the lesson it is.
- Feedback on written work should be encouraging and correction should aim to involve learners as far as possible.

CHAPTER

13 Commentary

Approaches to mistakes

Rebecca: This reflects a view that language learning is based on habit formation – often associated with behavioural psychology. Rebecca's view does **not** get much support from current research evidence, which suggests that mistakes are an inevitable part of the learning process.

Helen: Although there is much debate over just how useful correcting mistakes is, students tend to expect it and it is a fundamental part of the language teacher's job.

David: Many teachers would agree with David's position and certainly teachers should prioritise and correct important things (those that affect communication) before worrying too much about smaller details. However, if the details are never attended to, these may become ingrained and difficult for the learner to work on later.

Sophie: This reflects a view based more on a cognitive view of learning that mistakes are an inevitable (and useful) part of the learning process. Mistakes give an opportunity to help learners.

When to correct

I think I should correct every mistake.

Over-correction of every slip, every pronunciation problem and so on can dishearten students. It is important to prioritise. Start with the problems that interfere with meaning, and perhaps those that involve recently-presented language.

I try to correct most errors but I don't think it is important to correct slips.

An understandable position, but if the same slip goes uncorrected and therefore unnoticed by the student, it may become very hard to correct later. See the comments regarding David's views, above.

I would like to correct more but I find it hard to hear all the mistakes.

Nobody can hear everything that is said during pair and group work, but if teachers move around the room during these phases they can pick up on samples of language from lots of different sources. Typically learners speak more quietly during pair work than group work because they are physically closer to each other. So, if you have real problems hearing what they are saying, use more group work because learners are less likely to whisper to each other.

I correct more during accuracy phases of a lesson than fluency phases.

The amount of correction may not differ significantly between the two phases, but the timing of correction (instant or delayed – see Ways of correcting learners) often will be different.

I sometimes can't correct the learner because I can't work out what she was trying to say!

In these circumstances you need to try to negotiate the meaning with the learner, perhaps by asking appropriate questions (Do you mean...?) and then help the student say what they want to in a less ambiguous/confusing way.

I always try to let the learner who made the mistake correct herself before I do.

It is generally good to involve learners in the correction process, just as it is in any other part of the lesson.

If the learner who made the mistake can't correct herself then I ask if another learner can.

As above, it is generally good to involve learners, but you need to ensure that it is done with sensitivity (or at least, without any hint of mocking). This is rarely a problem in adult classes.

I never just say 'that's wrong' – I always try to show the learner which bit of what they said was wrong.

This is an important point. Take the following exchange:

Student: A few weeks ago I sawed a good movie.
Teacher: No, not quite.
Student: A little time ago I sawed a good movie.

This exchange is made up but it illustrates the point that if you do not highlight where the mistake is, the student may not necessarily locate it. S/he needs guidance on where the mistake is and/or the type of mistake made (vocabulary, pronunciation etc.).

I often feel awkward correcting learners – it seems so wrong because I can't speak their languages at all and I don't want to embarrass them.

It's true that you should be sensitive in the way in which you correct learners, but don't forget that most students expect the teacher to do this and feel that the teacher is letting them down if correction doesn't take place.

Are there any occasions when you should not correct?

1 ***When a new student in the class speaks for the first time.***
This is a sensible time not to correct, or at least to only do it very gently, perhaps by reformulating (repeating in a correct form) what the learner says – the emphasis should be on making her feel welcome and at ease in the class. It is a chance, though, for the teacher to gauge language level and any areas that may need attention in coming lessons.

2 ***When a learner is communicating something which is very important to them. For example, that they have just broken up with their partner.***
Inappropriate to correct.

3 ***When you are doing an activity of which the main aim is to help the group relax and enjoy the following parts of the lesson.***
Inappropriate to correct (because correction can increase stress) but still useful diagnostic information can be gained.

4 ***The teacher is angry with the learner because they are being disruptive.***
Although this may be a very human reaction as the teacher attempts to reassert power, it would be better to deal with the source and cause of the disruption.

5 ***When you are conducting feedback on a reading or listening text and although the learner says the correct answer s/he makes a small grammar mistake in doing so.***
Correction here can sometimes blur the focus of the lesson when there are a lot of short answers to get through and is therefore often not a good idea in these circumstances.

Ways of correcting learners

Fluency activities

1 Who corrects the mistakes? – the learners

2 What would the alternative be if this strategy were unsuccessful? – if the learners were unable to correct the mistake the teacher would do it.

3 What is the advantage of delaying the correction until after the activity? – the focus of the activity – the communication – continues uninterrupted.

Accuracy activities

a) ignore the mistake.
In an accuracy-based activity correcting mistakes is very important because the focus is on using the language forms correctly, therefore this is not a good idea.

b) say 'Yesterday we went to the beach'.
Learners are probably more likely to remember the new language if they are involved in the correction process. 'Reformulation' of this kind (where the teacher says the correct version) is often unnoticed by the learners and therefore may have little impact on their learning.

c) say 'in the past, so...'
This prompts the learner to correct herself. If she is unable to do so, the teacher could ask another member of the class – thereby ensuring that the whole class remains involved in the activity.

Match the gestures with the mistakes:
1 B **2** A **3** C

1 ***The teacher repeats the utterance up to the mistake.***
This is quick and easy but learners can sometimes misunderstand the intention of the teacher. If this is to be used it's a good idea to accompany it with an exaggerated intonation pattern or gesture.

2 ***The teacher tells the learner the correct form.***
This is quick and easy but the learner may not even realise they are being corrected. The learner does not need to put in any effort and therefore it may not be a memorable learning experience.

3 ***The teacher indicates where the error is by using a grammar term.***

This can be very useful as long as the teacher keeps to a very limited range of grammar terms that the learners understand.

Pronunciation

1 B **2** C **3** A

Giving feedback on written work

As well as the detailed feedback (see below) the teacher may also comment on the absence of paragraphing. However, the message, despite mistakes, communicates effectively and this should be praised.

There are quite a large number of mistakes here and the teacher may want to consider whether they are all worth drawing to the attention of the learner at this time because she may benefit more from focusing on a few priority areas. This, amongst other things, may depend on the expectations and needs of the individual learner.

Dear Sir/Madam

Sp G
I am writting to ask for some informations.
Sp T
My English is not perfect but I am studing English
Sp WW
for several years in a large langauge school at
\+ WW
Santiago, Chile. I want take a exam in the nearest
T
future. I do not do any English exams before. If
WW +
possible I would like to have IELTS exam. I would like
WO
to know how many parts does the exam consist of?
WW G
Should I registrate in advance? How much is it
WW
costs? I am also interesting in some practice
G P
material. Can you give me any advices. Please send
\+
me all necessary detail. Thank you for your help. I
\+
look forward to hear from you.

WW
Yours sincerely

Alejandra Gomez

CHAPTER 14

Developing learner independence

This chapter will look at ways in which learners can be helped to study on their own – without the direct involvement of a teacher.

Some arguments for developing learner independence

Look at the following statements and say if you agree or disagree with them.

	Agree	Disagree
There can never be enough classroom time for learners to learn everything they need to.		
Learners often have a better idea of what they want to study than teachers.		
Learners usually already know how to use dictionaries and reference books effectively.		
Learners need to be with a teacher to learn effectively.		

Learner independence is sometimes referred to as learner autonomy. Most learners, and nearly all teachers, rightly feel that language learning takes time, and often considerable amounts of it. No matter how hard the learners work in class time, they simply will not be able to make the progress they would like without working outside of this. Homework has often been seen as a way of achieving this, and there is certainly a place for it in most teaching contexts.

The notion of learner independence, however, moves beyond a traditional idea of completing homework tasks set by the teacher, and into an area where the learners can direct their own learning. It could be defined as those learning activities which take place without the immediate intervention of the teacher. Learners set their own objectives and follow strategies devised by themselves to fulfil them.

There are certain skills and strategies which can help to bring about successful learning, but these may not be known to all the learners. Therefore it is important that class time provides useful models of learning techniques, and in some cases provides explicit training for the learners, in order to help them become more efficient and effective when they study independently. Therefore the fostering of learner independence may start in a classroom environment and then extend beyond it.

It can also be argued that, once provided with the skills of how to learn effectively, learners will be able to choose to focus on the things that they consider to be important for their linguistic development – in other words each individual in a class may have different reasons for learning and different priorities and these can be catered for, to some extent at least, in their autonomous study. For example, a learner who has particular problems with pronunciation (which are not shared by the rest of the class) could focus on improving in this area outside class time. Learners can also use material which they find intrinsically interesting. A learner who likes music could read about their favourite bands, for example.

A further benefit of developing learner independence is that learners are forced to take some responsibility for their own learning. Some learners can be lulled into thinking that as long as they attend lessons, then language proficiency will follow. However, most teachers would argue that simply giving language to a learner is not within their power – the learner must be active in the process. This is true both inside and outside the classroom. One of the attractions of learner independence is that such an approach demands learner involvement and it is argued that such involvement will lead to a deeper and 'better' learning.

A further argument is that language learning is often thought of as an ongoing process. A language cannot be considered to have been learned at the end of a course of study because there will always be more for the learner to learn, and if language is not used it will almost certainly decay and the communicative competence of the learner will diminish. It is argued that if good learning skills are in place, then this ongoing process of learning can continue after the course of study as long as the learner is prepared to do the necessary work.

The extent to which such learner independence is possible will depend on the context in which the teaching is taking place. For example, learners who only have one or two hours of formal tuition a week may need to develop their ability to study independently as a priority, but others, many younger learners for example, may find the demands of autonomy difficult.

Classroom examples

Look at the activities below and answer the questions that follow.

Activity A

A class has read a short text and the teacher asks the learners to underline four words they do not know. The learners then look the words up in a dictionary. The teacher asks them to write down for each word:
- the meaning
- the part of speech (noun, verb etc.)
- an example sentence (taken from the original text, or the dictionary)
- a guide to the pronunciation of the word

She also tells the students that they can write a translation of the word, if they wish to.

1 Do you think this is a good use of classroom time?

2 What do the students learn? What skills do they develop?

Activity B

The school has a collection of graded readers (books which have been simplified so that they are appropriate for learners studying at lower levels). The teacher produces a table, listing the books vertically down one side and the learners' names going across horizontally. The learners take a book to read at home and when they have finished it, they give it a rating (1-5) and write a brief comment summarising what the book was about, what they enjoyed about the book and so on. Before making their next choice, the learner reads the comments of the previous readers.

3 What are the advantages of the teacher encouraging the learners to read in their own time?

Activity C

The teacher decides on a grammar point that she wants the class to learn, such as the differences between *so* and *such*. She asks the whole class to go home and find out about this grammar point and also to find a practice exercise.

4 What skills will the learners need to complete this task?

When you are ready, check your answers on page 100.

The above activities are all classroom-based and aim to help learners to develop skills so that they can study effectively when they are not with a teacher. We will move on to look at other strategies that learners can use.

Working outside the classroom

Imagine that you are teaching a class and learners want advice on how they could practise more outside the classroom. Think about the following questions.

1 How can learners develop speaking skills outside the class?

2 How can learners develop listening skills outside the class?

3 How can learners practise writing skills outside the class?

4 How might learners be able to use the internet to practise their English?

When you are ready, check your answers on page 100.

One of the easiest ways for learners to practise their English is to find a written text to read. Simply reading the text will help learners' reading skills and the exposure to natural English may also be beneficial. Simply seeing words in context may help with vocabulary acquisition, but there are other straightforward strategies that learners could use which may promote more active learning. Here are some ideas to develop vocabulary awareness suggested by different learners.

Anja's idea

I read a text and write definitions of new words (from a dictionary) but I do **not** write the new word down. I try to remember the word that goes with the definition the next day. If I can't, I re-read the text and try the exercise again. If I do remember the word I write it down, although I sometimes wait to see if I can remember it after two or three days.

David's idea

I copy out the sentences from the text that have a new word in but in place of the new word I leave a gap. '*John _____ breaking the window*'. Later I go back and try to fill in the gaps.

Cristina's idea

I read a text and write down some of the important and new words. I try to write a summary of the text and use the new words. When I have finished the summary I check back and look to see if I used the words in the same way as in the original text. I can usually see if I have made a mistake and misunderstood the word.

Roman's idea

I read the text really quickly and decide on what it is about and some categories associated with it. I am a biology student and yesterday I read about an experiment. I made up three categories – words to describe the experiment, words to do with cells, and words to do with organs of the body. I then re-read the text and put all the words I could find into the best group.

It seems that all of these activities worked for the learners concerned. They may, or may not, appeal to other learners but it is often a good idea for a teacher to spend a few minutes talking to learners about the strategies they use to study, because other learners can often use the ideas they hear about.

The role of the teacher

In Chapter 2 we looked at some of the roles that teachers need to perform. One of those we termed 'expert guide' – where the teacher helps the learners to see rules and patterns for themselves. This is the start of helping learners to become more independent and less reliant on the teacher. A learner who is used to being told everything by the teacher is unlikely to develop a great deal of independence. Some learners would like to study more but cannot pinpoint their own needs or weaknesses. In these cases the teacher needs to be prepared to give guidance on what things the learner may benefit from studying. If time allows, a short individual tutorial with a learner can be very beneficial.

In the classroom teaching context we said that the teacher had to provide appropriate input for the learners. In developing learner independence there is a parallel role, in that the teacher needs to make learners aware of sources of appropriate material for them to access. In some cases they may need to provide some training on how to exploit this material to the best effect.

The teacher may also need to be a motivating force for learners to continue their studies outside the classroom and to provide tasks to support this. For example, learners could be asked to complete a short journal entry every few weeks in which they describe what steps they have taken to learn language outside the classroom and how effective they feel it has been. Such journals can also provide feedback to the teacher on which learners may need more support and guidance before they can become more fully independent.

Summary

- Classroom time is very limited in most teaching/learning contexts and independent learning helps to alleviate these constraints.
- Learners can focus on what is relevant and interesting to them as individuals.
- Learners can develop skills that will allow them to continue learning after a particular course has ended.
- Teachers need to teach in a way that helps to foster independence and in some cases teach the specific skills required.

CHAPTER 14 Commentary

Classroom examples

Activity A

1 Do you think this is a good use of classroom time?

2 What do the students learn? What skills do they develop?

Although it may seem that this is a rather slow way of teaching just a few items of vocabulary, the time may be well spent in the long run. By spending a relatively small amount of classroom time helping learners to see the range of information available in the dictionary, and how to construct good vocabulary records, the teacher is helping the learners to develop the skills to be effective learners outside the classroom.

The teacher could also advise learners that it is a good idea to group words thematically. For example, when a learner finds a new word to do with crime, it is a good idea to group it with other words relating to crime. It seems that the mind stores words which have related meanings together.

Activity B

3 What are the advantages of the teacher encouraging the learners to read in their own time?

Obviously reading skills should improve, but also exposure to English is useful and reading (at an appropriate level) is a good way of learners increasing their exposure to the language. It seems likely that if they come across words and patterns enough times in contexts that they understand, then learners are likely to remember these things, without necessarily making a great deal of conscious effort.

Activity C

4 What skills will the learners need to complete this task?

In order to successfully do this task, learners will need to use a grammar reference book effectively (or some other source, such as one on the internet). They will also have to find an appropriate practice exercise. By doing this they demonstrate that they have the skills to find out about grammar and then to practise what they have learned. These are skills that are very important if the learners are to be able to work independently. Again, the benefit of the task is less in what the learners find out about this particular grammar point, and more to do with the skills they develop in doing it. It should be noted that learners will almost certainly need to understand basic terminology used to describe language because most 'rules' on form and meaning are framed in these terms.

Working outside the classroom

1 ***How can learners develop speaking skills outside the class?***

Ideally learners will find opportunities to speak to others who wish to practise. They may speak to classmates, or former classmates, or join clubs. Of course, if they are in an English speaking environment then there should be plenty of opportunities. However, if such opportunities do not exist, there are still ways of practising. Some learners have reported that they feel a benefit in speaking to themselves in English – for example, trying to construct a commentary on what they are doing. Learners can also make tapes of themselves speaking English and this can help them to develop accuracy because they can later check what they have said. This is also a useful technique because learners should hear some progress if they compare early tapes with later ones.

2 ***How can learners develop listening skills outside the class?***

Some access to material is available in most places either through radio or satellite television. However, it is usually aimed at native speakers and can therefore be difficult for lower level learners, and graded material can be far harder to find. It can also be difficult for learners to know whether they have understood accurately. For this reason some like to combine listening and reading practice. By listening to a news bulletin and then reading about the same story (in a newspaper or on the internet), learners can sometimes get a better idea of whether they understood accurately.

3 ***How can learners practise writing skills outside the class?***

Obviously learners can produce writing but it can be difficult to find a reader, although it may be possible for learners to find a writing partner to correspond with. The internet does allow for learners, along with everyone else, to contribute to discussion boards, chat rooms and so on, although this is a fairly limited type of writing. Again, if the teacher can instil good practice in the classroom then this may help learners to learn independently outside it. For example, good writers are generally able to look at what they have written, spot their own mistakes and correct them. This is a skill which learners can continue to practise whether or not they are in a classroom.

4 ***How might learners be able to use the internet to practise their English?***

In the above discussion we have already mentioned the use of the internet as a source of language from which learners can learn. There are sites which are useful for specific language practice, such as providing grammar and vocabulary exercises and other related material. A simple search on the internet, such as 'English grammar practice' will yield many results. In teaching contexts where technology is available to the whole class, the teacher may usefully help learners to discover what is available in class time and then encourage them to use it more in their own time.

However, learners can also make use of a whole range of other sites that are not specifically designed to give language practice. For example, they can place messages on discussion boards or enter chat rooms to improve more spontaneous communication. It can be difficult for students who are shy to find opportunities to practise spontaneous language production, but chat rooms may be a good way of starting. They are reasonably anonymous, and this may help shy learners, and many learners are more confident of their typing speed than their speaking ability. Despite the obvious differences, this is a possible early step in reasonably spontaneous language use.

Learners can also find, for example, reviews of films they have seen, or books they have read (either in English or their own language). The knowledge they have of the subject will help their comprehension. A similar opportunity exists with news stories. The BBC web site, for example, has news in 43 languages. This allows most learners to find and read a story in their own language and then read the English version, or to read the English version and then check their understanding by reading it in their own language.

The internet offers rich opportunities for learners to improve their language skills, although they may find one or two suggestions from their teachers helpful in the first instance.

CHAPTER

15 Learner variation

All classes contain learners of mixed levels of English language ability, although the extent of the differences will vary considerably in different teaching contexts. In state systems classes may be formed on the basis of age, rather than language level, and in small private language schools there may only be the capacity for three or four classes, making the range of level in each potentially quite great.

Even if at the beginning of a period of teaching the learners all seem to have a roughly equivalent level of English, it is not long before differences begin to emerge. The differences are not just linguistic, of course, because learners bring with them different experiences, needs and expectations. Any class is made up of individuals and a teacher needs to keep sight of this as far as possible.

There are lots of reasons why different learners will learn at different rates. In this chapter we will look at some of the reasons for these differences in learner progress.

Read about each situation and try to answer the questions that follow.

When you are ready, check your answers on page 105.

Age

A class of 6- and 7-year-olds is working in groups and each group has an outline drawing of a robot. The children are cutting up coloured paper and sticking the pieces onto the outline. The teacher circulates and speaks to the children in English. She encourages them to use English to ask for scissors, more paper and so on, and also to talk to other people in the group. The teacher frequently talks to the children about the colours they are using.

1 Do you think that children are better at learning languages than adults?

2 Assuming this is a typical lesson, is the course similar in structure to one that would be used for adults? (That is to say, the children have a course with lots of activities, but very little overt teaching, particularly of grammar.)

For more on teaching young learners, see Chapter 17.

Motivation

In a class of fifteen young adult learners there are people with different reasons for trying to learn English. Here are some examples:

Cinzia is a doctor. She needs to learn to read medical journals written in English, and also she occasionally attends conferences at which English is the dominant language. She sees English as an essential way of furthering her career.

Elizabetta works in sales. She uses English to communicate with many of the important clients she deals with on a daily basis. Her company has sent her on the course, although she is not sure she needs to improve her English.

Carlo loves English culture and visits England as often as possible. He is desperate to learn as much English as he can so that he can talk to people more easily when he visits.

3 In what ways are Cinzia and Elizabetta similarly motivated? In what ways are they different?

4 How is Carlo's motivation different to that of Cinzia and Elizabetta?

Personality

In a class of young adults a teacher notices that some students tend to dominate the lesson. They are always quick to answer questions, and during pair and group work tend to say a lot more than their colleagues. Some learners are far more passive and don't speak very much at all.

5 In what areas of language learning would you expect more extrovert people to do well?

6 To what extent should the teacher try to ensure that everyone participates an equal amount?

Learning styles

When a teacher presents new language to the class she notices that some learners immediately want to see the language written down. Others want to say the new language several times and even mumble it to themselves. Some learners seem more interested when they have the opportunity to use the language in a role play. Some learners seem not to enjoy role play and taking on characters and views that they do not personally hold. Instead they prefer discussion activities, where they can voice their own opinions.

7 Which of the strategies outlined above is closest to your own preferred learning style?

8 In a classroom situation, what can a teacher do to help all the learners and their preferred styles?

First language background

In a mixed nationality class of 16 learners, a teacher notices that certain patterns emerge. There are three Arab learners in the class and although they communicate effectively when speaking, their writing is very inaccurate and their reading slow. Two Thai learners have problems when speaking because others find their pronunciation hard to understand. The Italian and French learners often seem able to guess what words mean and this helps their reading and listening.

9 Why might Arab learners find reading and writing difficult?

10 Why might French and Italian learners be able to guess what words mean?

11 Why might English pronunciation be harder for some learners than others?

12 In a mixed nationality class, to what extent can a teacher help learners from different backgrounds?

We have looked at age, motivation, personality traits, learning styles and first language background. There are other factors which may also affect success in learning, such as educational background. If someone has learned successfully before, particularly learned languages well, then it may be assumed that they are likely to do better in a classroom situation than someone who has had little classroom based education. In some cases, particularly in the case of those forced to leave their country, it may be that some learners will not have had the opportunity to learn to read and write in their own language. Clearly this will impact on the speed at which they develop these skills in a second language.

Many people would argue that some learners simply have a greater **aptitude** for learning language than others and this may well be the case. It is often assumed that this aptitude will be linked to intelligence (in the sense of what is measured in an IQ test). Learners with a high IQ do tend to do well in situations where the focus of the teaching is on grammar rules and the patterns behind the language. However, it seems less of a factor in success when a greater emphasis is placed on oral communication. In these contexts a learner's IQ is a less reliable indicator of potential success in learning.

Implications for teaching

Not all the factors mentioned are open to teacher influence. The teacher cannot change the age of the learners, but the teacher can vary his/her teaching style to suit the needs and expectations of the learners. The teacher cannot change the personalities of the learners, but can ensure that the classroom feels a relaxed and friendly environment so that language can be practised and used in a non-threatening atmosphere. It is generally argued that learners will do best when they are free from anxiety and feel secure in their environment. Teachers need to develop strategies which develop the learners' self esteem, allow them to participate when they wish, and allow them to experiment with language use in such a protected environment. The teacher needs to consider strategies to achieve this. They may include adopting sensitive correction techniques, the use of background music, respecting cultural differences and above all treating the learners with respect at all times.

Teachers cannot make the learners want to learn, but they can influence a learner's motivation. Clearly if a learner does not want to learn a language and has negative feelings towards a language, there is little the teacher can do. However, by trying to cater for the needs of the group, and making lessons relevant and interesting for learners, teachers can help to build and retain motivation. The topics chosen can play a big part in this, and learners can be involved in discussions on lesson content to ensure that the material meets their needs and is of interest. Careful monitoring of individuals, personalised goals and so on can also boost motivation. Teachers also need to remember that learners will generally respond well to praise, and correction needs to be carried out sensitively.

Similarly, teachers cannot change the preferred learning styles of learners, but they can ensure that a variety of styles, visual, auditory, involving movement and so on are catered for, by ensuring that varied input material is used.

Summary

- The case that young learners have a big advantage over others has not been proved conclusively.
- The more distant the first language is from English, the harder learners are likely to find learning.
- Motivation is an essential part of successful language learning and is open to some teacher influence.
- Extroverts may do well in oral fluency activities.
- Learners will have different preferences for how they learn.

CHAPTER

15 Commentary

Age

1 It is a fairly common assumption that age is a major factor in language learning. People often argue that children find learning languages 'easy' and that as we get older more effort is required and results are never as good. Although the research evidence may not be entirely conclusive, there are reasons to challenge this assumption. The argument that young children are better learners than others is strongest when phonological features of a second language are considered. The children of immigrant families often speak with an accent which is much closer to, or even indistinguishable from, that of a native speaker. Their parents, on the other hand, rarely achieve such levels. However, it could be argued that the differences in performance in such situations are a result of variables other than age. Children may have more opportunities (through school) to hear models of native speaker language. Another factor may be that their parents have a stronger desire to preserve their identity and therefore do not wish to imitate native speakers perfectly.

There is some evidence that, particularly in classroom settings, children are quite inefficient language learners. For most children who study a language at school for just a few hours a week there is little evidence that starting very young gives a lasting benefit.

2 While adult courses may include activities that allow spontaneous and fairly 'unstructured' communication, there is often a greater emphasis on more overt teaching of grammar and vocabulary. This may partly be because of learner expectation. Most teachers also feel that complicated grammar explanations are inappropriate for young learners because of the cognitive demands of understanding abstract grammar patterns. Therefore courses for young learners are often more activity based.

Motivation

3 Both Cinzia and Elizabetta are learning English because it may help career prospects. Elizabetta's motivation may not be as strong as Cinzia's because the decision to take the course was not her own.

4 Carlo's motivation is different in that he sees English as a means of accessing a culture that he likes.

Most people agree that motivation is an extremely important factor in language learning. Teachers can only help learners to learn, they cannot make them. Although intuitively all teachers realise that motivation is key, it remains a difficult thing to investigate.

One problem for researchers is the symbiotic relationship between success in learning and motivation. We may assume that motivation leads to success, but it is equally plausible that successful learning produces motivation. People are motivated to do the things that they are good at. The likelihood is that a virtuous circle is created whereby successful learning produces motivation which leads to further success and so on.

Researchers usually separate motivation into categories. The terminology used varies slightly in different studies but the broad distinctions are usually similar. We will use the fairly common terms of '**integrative**' motivation and '**instrumental**' motivation.

Integrative motivation refers to a desire to learn English in order become part of (or integrate with) an English speaking community. In some contexts, where a language is forced on a population for political purposes, for example, learners may have a very negative feeling towards the language and what it represents, and this may affect their learning. Instrumental motivation refers to the desire to learn English as a means of achieving something else. For example, it may be that a good command of English will open opportunities to study, or possibilities of promotion. Of course, human beings are complex and most learners may have a mixture of motivations for learning a language. In the above examples, Cinzia and Elizabetta would seem to have instrumental motivation to learn, while Carlo's is more integrative.

However, motivation does not account for success on its own. It could be argued that those who are desperate to learn a language sometimes place undue pressure on themselves and this can create barriers to learning in the form of high stress levels. Even in classes where everyone seems very motivated, there is still likely to be differences in the rate of progress achieved.

Personality

5 It may be that more outgoing people gain more attention from the teacher and get more practice opportunities in the classroom. It is argued that extroverts may also be more willing to take risks and be more prepared to try out language skills – usually associated with being an aid to learning. Therefore extroverts may be more likely to do better in measurements of speaking ability. However, although shy people may do less well in oral fluency activities they may perform better in written communication and in assessments which test grammatical understanding. Again, it should be stressed that these are broad distinctions and teachers should be wary of over-generalising.

6 A teacher needs to respect personality differences but also try to avoid inappropriate domination of the class by a small part of the group. Everyone should have the opportunity to speak, but this does not necessarily mean that everyone must speak.

Learning styles

7 Answers will vary.

8 There are people who feel that they understand and remember things when they see them, others who like to hear them, others who like to translate things. There are learners who will equate language learning with a knowledge of grammar rules, and others who will want to communicate as much as possible in lessons. Some learners like to be still and quiet and listen to the teacher speak, while others like to move around and be more active.

This can be difficult for teachers because we tend to assume that everyone learns in a similar way to ourselves and there is a tendency to teach in the way that we feel we ourselves learn. A teacher who herself responds well to visual input needs to guard against allowing this kind of input to dominate all that she does. If people learn in different ways then lessons must have variety in order to allow for the different learning styles found in any one class. Teachers may advise learners on different learning strategies but need to be wary of being overly dogmatic about a single way of learning. Teachers need to be aware of potentially different styles and try to cater for them by including varied input.

First language background

9 Arabic writing runs from right to left. Arab learners must learn an entirely new alphabet and new conventions, such as the use of capital letters. Learners who do not use the Roman alphabet in their first language (as English does) are likely to find reading much more difficult than others because they have to decode the shapes of letters and words in a way that other learners do automatically. They may also find copying notes from the board harder, and may copy less accurately if there is a time pressure.

10 In French, Italian, Spanish and Portuguese many words are derived from Latin, just as a number of English words are. These words often look similar and are often used in similar ways in all these languages.

11 Again this is a question of the degree of difference that exists between languages. If a learner's language has markedly different stress and intonation patterns, for example, they are likely to find English pronunciation harder in these areas. Also if individual sounds in English do not exist in a learner's mother tongue, then these too are likely to cause difficulty.

12 The teacher needs to remember that learners will have different needs. These can be catered for in various ways. One of these is to develop learner independence (see Chapter 14) – the teacher can guide and counsel the learners and allow them the time to work on areas of particular difficulty independently. In extreme cases the teacher may want to 'differentiate' material so that different learners have different tasks to do. For example, in a writing lesson, learners who find writing extremely difficult could be given a series of sentences to join together, while learners who are better at writing construct a paragraph for themselves.

CHAPTER

16 Planning and example lesson plans

For new or inexperienced teachers planning often involves the 'here and now' and the asking of such questions as: 'What am I going to teach next? How can I teach it? Where can I find suitable material?' This is natural, although planning also involves lessons further into the future and such questions as: 'How long is the course? What needs to be included? What weighting should be given to the different components of the course? What sequence should those components be taught in?'

The degree to which it is desirable, and indeed possible, to plan a long way into the future will vary greatly from teaching context to teaching context. Some schools have an intake of new students every week, making long term planning impossible. In other cases learners may enrol for a year or more, or courses may have been run before, allowing for quite detailed planning.

We will look first at the planning of individual lessons.

Reasons for planning

Look at the following statements and number them 1-4, where 1 is the most important.

- ☐ A good teacher should know their subject.
- ☐ A good teacher should make lessons interesting.
- ☐ A good teacher should plan their lessons carefully.
- ☐ A good teacher should respond to the needs of individuals.

There is of course no one correct answer for this and it could be argued that they all involve planning, making it impossible to compare this to the other three points. Most people when asked about the qualities of a good teacher include that they should 'know their subject'. For a new teacher of languages this can seem daunting. Native speakers in particular are often unaware of the 'rules' that can be extracted from the language that they use so naturally and to try to teach them to others can cause anxiety. However, thorough planning can help to alleviate the stress of this. It may be that the teacher can only prepare the small part of language that will be taught in a given lesson but at least for the purposes of that lesson some kind of expertise can be obtained.

Learners also feel that lessons should be interesting. Again, careful planning can help to achieve this. It may be that the material you have to use seems uninspiring but careful preparation may allow the teacher to think of more interesting ways of 'selling' it to the learners, or allow the teacher the opportunity to supplement the material with something more intrinsically interesting.

It is undoubtedly true that good teachers should respond to individuals. Teachers should remember that they need to teach the people in the class, rather than the plan they have prepared. This calls for some flexibility and a willingness to divert from the plan when it becomes necessary. To some extent flexibility can be built in at the planning stage. For example, a teacher may prepare two practice activities – one relatively more difficult than the other – and then decide to use whichever one s/he feels is more appropriate as the lesson proceeds.

In the light of the above, look at the following comments on planning made by experienced teachers. Try to think of the reasons behind each comment.

Tracy: *The best lessons are the ones that I don't plan at all.*

Jenny: *It's exhausting. I'm planning lessons until about 10.30 at night.*

Gary: *I try to plan a bit for each lesson but I usually end up changing it.*

Alex: *If I don't have a plan for the lesson then it soon becomes total chaos. I have to plan carefully.*

When you are ready, read the commentary on page 117.

Planning is an important part of teaching. As well as helping the flow and progression of an individual lesson, careful planning can help teachers to feel more confident, and this confidence can lead to teachers performing with more conviction and authority. To write an effective plan the teacher needs to think carefully about what exactly the aim of the lesson is. What will the learners learn? Once the learning outcome is clear, the teacher should ensure that all the stages of the lesson contribute to achieving that aim. We will now go on to look at some example lesson plans.

Example lesson plans

In the following plans the activity column refers to learner and teacher activity - what happens in the classroom. The rationale column explains **why** this has been planned. The interaction column indicates who is interacting with whom. It may be the teacher with the students or students talking to each other, for example. The first column gives a name to each section of the lesson and an indication of how long each section will take.

There is no right or wrong way to plan lessons. Some institutions will have their own format of plan which they will expect teachers to follow, and how much detail is included is often a matter of personal choice.

Vocabulary – 50 minutes (The material for this lesson is reproduced in Appendix 4)		Intermediate level Aim: Learners understand and have the chance to practise expressions using the word 'heart'.	
Stage/Time	**Activity**	**Interaction**	**Rationale**
0-5 Warmer	Teacher draws a heart on the board. Learners discuss what they associate with the image and any expressions using (a translation of) 'heart' they have in their own language.	st-st	to introduce the lesson and raise interest in subject matter
6-12 Focus on meaning	Learners match examples of use to definitions (individually). Learners compare answers in pairs. Feedback	 st-st sts-t	to ensure that learners understand the meaning of the expressions and have a record of how they are used in a sentence to build confidence to ensure learners have the correct answers
13-18 Practice 1	Learners answer the questions as quickly as possible. Feedback	 sts-t	to check learners have understood how the expressions are used to ensure learners have the correct answers
19-25 Practice 2	Learners work in two groups, A and B, and complete the gaps in their questions. Teacher monitors and helps/corrects as necessary.	sts-sts	to give further practice to ensure learners have the correct answers
26-38 Practice 3	A learner from A works with one from B to ask and answer the questions. Feedback: learners report their conversations. Feedback: teacher corrects any mistakes heard.	st-st sts-t t-sts	to give further oral practice and to integrate new language with existing knowledge to round off the discussion and give further practice to focus on accuracy of use
39-50 Practice 4	Learners work individually to complete the sentences. Learners compare answers in pairs. Feedback	 st-st sts-t	to check that learners have understood the new expressions to build confidence to ensure learners have the correct answers

Reading – 50 minutes (The reading text for this lesson is reproduced on page 140.)		Pre-intermediate level Aim: Learners practise reading for gist and specific information.	
Stage/Time	**Activity**	**Interaction**	**Rationale**
0-4 Building interest	Teacher asks learners which animals make the best pets.	t-sts	to introduce the theme of the text and create interest in the text
5-12 Vocabulary focus	Teacher elicits/teaches essential vocabulary *blaze, cat flap, nominate, gutted* and writes it on the board.	t-sts sts-t	to make the text easier to understand for the learners
13-20 Prediction	Learners work in groups to predict content of story from vocabulary and headline. Learners report their predictions to the class	sts-sts sts-sts	to practise vocabulary and help with understanding the text by thinking in advance of content to set up following activity
21-24 Gist reading	Learners read (max. 2 mins.) to see whose prediction was closest to the story. Learners compare answers in pairs. Teacher checks answers.	st-text st-st t-sts	pre-set task creates a reason to read the text. Time limit creates the need to read quickly and therefore practise gist reading to build confidence to ensure answers are correct
25-35 Intensive reading	Teacher gives out intensive reading questions (see Chapter 8). Checks learners understand questions. Learners read and answer questions. Learners compare answers in pairs. Teacher checks answers.	t-sts st-text st-st t-sts	pre-set task creates a reason to read the text. to build confidence to ensure answers are correct
36-45 Extension activity	Learners work in groups to discuss the advantages and disadvantages of keeping pets.	sts-sts	to provide speaking/listening practice in the context of the text
46-50 Feedback	Learners report their discussions. Teacher highlights good examples of language used and also some mistakes.	sts-sts t-sts	to highlight the communicative value of the speaking to help learners improve and learn from mistakes

Writing – 50 minutes (The material for this lesson is reproduced in Appendix 4)		Pre-intermediate level Aim: Learners write short letters to and from a problem page.	
Stage/Time	**Activity**	**Interaction**	**Rationale**
0-4 Warmer	Teacher leads discussion on types of magazine and sections within them. Leads to problem page.	t-sts	to provide lead in to the theme of the lesson
5-12 Building context	Learners read three short letters to a problem page and match them to the responses. Learners compare answers Feedback to teacher	st-text st-st sts-t	texts are a model of the type of writing learners will later create to build confidence to ensure answers are correct
13-18 Language focus	Teacher focuses on some of the useful language in the letters and suggestion and advice structures	t-sts	to prepare learners for the following writing task
19-27 Writing 1	Learners work in pairs to make up and write a short problem letter. Teacher circulates and helps where necessary.	st-st	to practise writing skills to provide support and avoid learners making too many errors
28-40 Writing 2	Teacher collects the letters and redistributes to another pair. Learners read and then write a response. Teacher collects and returns 'advice' to orignial letter writers.	 st-st	to ensure that there is communication in the activity to practise writing skills
41-45 Feedback 1	Teacher leads feedback on whether advice was thought to be useful.	sts-t	to highlight the communicative value of the writing
46-50 Feedback 2	Teacher highlights good uses of language noticed during the lesson and some mistakes.	t-sts	to help learners improve and learn from mistakes

Grammar – 50 minutes		Intermediate level Aim: to present and practise *used to* + infinitive to refer to past habits and states (to a class of adult learners).	
Stage/Time	**Activity**	**Interaction**	**Rationale**
0-10 Discussion	The teacher introduces the theme of the lesson – schooldays – and gives learners the following prompts – *discipline, uniform, play time*. Learners sit quietly to think of what they want to say about the prompts, and use dictionaries or ask the teacher questions. Learners then work in groups of three to discuss their schooldays.	t-sts sts-sts	to give learners ideas of what they could talk about to give learners a chance to think of vocabulary they need and gather some ideas to practise communicating about the past
11-17 Model of language use	Teacher plays a tape of English people doing the same activity. Learners fill in gaps in the tapescript.	sts-text	gaps focus on *used to* and draw attention to its use in context
18-21 Focus on form	The teacher writes an example sentence from the tapescript and highlights the form on the board.	t-sts	to ensure learners understand the form
22-25 Checking understanding	Learners look at the example *We used to play football in the playground* and answer the following questions: Is this about the past or the present? (*past*) Did the speaker play once or many times? (*many*) Teacher checks answers	t-sts	to ensure learners understand the meaning of *used to*
26-40 Discussion 2	The teacher gives learners the following prompts – *teachers, friends* and *hours/times/ages* Learners sit quietly to think of what they want to say about the prompts and use dictionaries or ask the teacher questions. Learners then work in groups of three to discuss their schooldays.	sts-sts	to give learners ideas of what they could talk about to give learners a chance to think of vocabulary they need and gather some ideas to practise communicating about the past and give the opportunity to use the new language introduced
41-45 Feedback 1	Teacher leads feedback on the discussion	sts-t	to highlight the communicative value of the speaking
46-50 Feedback 2	Teacher highlights good uses of language noticed during the lesson and some mistakes.	t-sts	to help learners improve and learn from mistakes

Lesson planning checklists

As teachers gain experience so planning gets easier. However, particularly when you start teaching, having a checklist of things you need to think about for each type of lesson can be useful. Look at the types of lesson in the table below and put the questions from the box into the appropriate columns. Some questions can go in more than one box. The first has been done as an example.

Vocabulary and grammar	Receptive skills (reading and listening)	Productive skills (speaking and writing)
	Is there a lead in to the topic?	Is there a lead in to the topic?

- Is there a lead in to the topic?
- Are there sufficient and varied practice opportunities?
- How will the meaning of the new language be conveyed?
- Have interaction patterns been considered?
- Will the teacher/activity dictate the form and content of what is produced, or will the learners be free to produce the language they want?
- Has the form been covered adequately?
- Will learner understanding of the new language be checked?
- Is there enough/too much new language?
- How will language errors be dealt with?
- Are there clear tasks and will they be set before the learners see the text?
- Has the language been presented in a common context or contexts?
- Is there too much new vocabulary in the text?
- Will the focus be on fluency, accuracy or both?
- Will learners have the opportunity to discuss answers?
- Would using time limits for tasks be helpful?
- Has the meaning been covered adequately?
- How will problems in understanding be dealt with?

When you are ready, compare your answer with the one on page 117.

Planning a series of lessons

As well as planning individual lessons, teachers also need to consider how lessons fit together. Lessons cannot exist in isolation because the language from one lesson will impact on what needs to be covered, or can be covered, in future lessons. New language, for example, needs to be recycled, giving learners the best possible chance to acquire it. In addition, learners need to feel that they are getting a unified and organised course rather than a series of one-off and unrelated lessons.

In some cases the shape of the course can be quite easily defined, because there will be a syllabus in place which has been drawn up by a government department, exam board or some other institution which is beyond the control of the teacher. However, in some cases the teacher may be left to determine much of the content of the course themselves. In these cases the main consideration when planning a series of lessons is what the learners need to learn. Needs are not always easy to identify and teachers often use a technique called a '**needs analysis**' to help. A needs analysis is essentially a string of questions that the learner answers which may cover such things as why they need English, whether they spend relatively more time speaking English than writing it and so on. The degree of detail can vary enormously from one needs analysis to another. The degree of detail you need will depend on the amount of flexibility you have in tailoring the plan to the learners. Some learners have a very clear idea of why they are learning English and exactly what their needs are, while others have only a vague idea of the situations in which they may be called upon to use the language. The learners in any one class may have quite different needs to each other and the larger the class is the more divergent these needs are likely to be. The teacher has to try to juggle the different needs within the class by providing a balance of what the different individuals would like from their course. Teachers should also remember that needs can change over a period of time and they therefore need to be prepared to review the needs of the learners at regular intervals. A simple needs analysis form is included in Appendix 4.

However the course content is decided upon, the teacher is often left to put the pieces into a clear and logical order. Imagine you are teaching a 24-hour course. The learners will study for 3 hours a day for eight days. You decide that the course should include the following:

- grammar
- vocabulary
- listening practice
- speaking practice
- reading practice
- writing practice
- language games
- listening to songs

Colleagues make the following five suggestions – say whether you think they are good ideas or not.

	Good idea	Not a good idea
1 Devote one day to each of the course components.		
2 Use songs and games on a Friday afternoon.		
3 Devote the first 90 minutes of each day to either grammar or vocabulary.		
4 Devote the second 90 minutes of each day to skills development work.		
5 Try to have a variety of activities in any one day.		

When you are ready, read the commentary on page 118.

Selecting material

What comes first, the plan or the material? This is a difficult question to resolve. In many ways it would seem logical that the plan, or at least the start of it, should come first – the teacher decides what should be taught and then finds suitable material. However, the reality for most teachers is that they have a course book which supplies most of the material used on the course. Teachers then select material from the book and plan accordingly.

There are both advantages and disadvantages to using course books. Look at the list of points below and separate them into advantages and disadvantages.

- Continual use of one book becomes dull.
- Course books save the teacher's time.
- Course books tend to adopt a conservative approach to language teaching and restrict experimentation.
- Course books provide a coherent course with a sense of progression.

- Course books recycle new language.
- No course book can reflect accurately the needs of a particular group.
- Course books are often produced for a mass market and ignore local needs and cultures.
- The book provides a record of the course for learners to use as reference.
- Course books grade material appropriately.

When you are ready, compare your answer to the one on page 118.

There are many advantages to using course books and most teachers are expected to use them. However, no materials writer can know a particular group of learners as well as their teacher and so the ultimate responsibility for choosing material must remain with the teacher. This means that the teacher needs to look at the material carefully and decide whether it fits in with the needs of the learners, their interests and so on. If it doesn't, then the material should not be used. The teacher must also ensure that there is sufficient variety of lesson type within the course.

Teachers can sometimes meet the needs of their learners better simply by adapting activities or material from the course book. For example, a reading text which has already been studied could be photocopied and the teacher could blank out the new vocabulary that was taught and then ask the learners to fill the gaps. This gives extra practice and recycles the vocabulary. If learners find the listening sections of a book difficult, the teacher could allow learners to listen with a transcript of the recorded material. (Transcripts are often supplied either in the learner's course book or in the teacher's edition.) If a teacher wants to highlight a particular language point, such as linking devices, s/he could copy a text from the book, cut it up and ask learners to put it back in the correct order. Learners could then highlight the linking words ('although', 'despite', 'however', 'in addition to' and so on) which allowed them to do this.

There are countless ways in which material can be adapted, but the starting point is always the teacher asking themselves 'Is this material useful for the learners?' and if it isn't, finding ways in which the needs are more successfully met.

Although teachers sometimes complain about the course book they are using, without them they would have to spend a lot more time finding appropriate material that was professionally presented, recycled new language and was graded to the level of their learners. It is worth remembering that very, very few course books are actually poor in themselves, but problems can arise when an inappropriate book is selected for a particular group of learners. Amongst other reasons, it may be inappropriate in terms of level, topics covered, approach to learning and teaching or assume too much, or too little, world knowledge.

Course books are generally a help to most teachers when they use them to meet the needs of the learners, but they can become a hindrance if the teacher allows the course book to dictate the course content without questioning the value of each activity to the people being taught.

Monitoring progress

Part of a teacher's job is to check that learners are making progress. Where an individual's progress is disappointing, advice can be given on alternative learning strategies, or in some cases extra work could be given. Often this monitoring can be done through simply being observant during lessons, looking at homework exercises, and so on.

However, sometimes it is useful to monitor progress in a slightly more objective and systematic way, and one of the easiest ways of doing this is to set the learners a test. Many course books have tests built into them at regular intervals. There are several advantages to testing learners. As well as the information the teacher gets about progress, learners often find them very motivating and also often expect to be tested as part of their course.

The following is a brief guide for teachers who need to design their own tests.

1 The test should reflect what has been taught. If the course has focused on, for example, speaking and listening skills, then these skills should be tested. It would be unfair to include a series of grammar questions. If the learners have been taught a lot of grammar then those grammar areas that have been taught should be included rather than **any** grammar.

2 The instructions for each activity should be very clear, giving examples where necessary. Otherwise there is a chance that the result will reflect a misinterpretation of the question, rather than poor language skills.

3 The test should be appropriate for the range of ability in the class. If it is too difficult, the learners will become discouraged, and if it is too easy neither the teacher nor the learners will learn anything of use.

4 A mark scheme should be devised which is clear and user friendly.

Teachers may want, or be required, to administer more formal tests. See Chapter 17 – Teaching exam classes – for guidance in this area.

Summary

- Careful planning is important – it can help to build confidence.
- Teachers should be flexible when implementing their plan.
- The starting point for the plan should be the main aim/objective of the lesson.
- When planning a series of lessons teachers should ensure that learners get a varied and balanced diet.
- Course books can help teachers enormously but teachers still need to evaluate each piece of material and decide if it will be useful for their group.
- Teachers need to monitor the progress of individuals in the group.

CHAPTER

16 Commentary

Reasons for planning

Tracy's view is expressed fairly frequently by teachers and there is no doubt that **some** unplanned lessons work well, partly because the lesson can sometimes develop a life and momentum of its own which the teacher manages to judge and control effectively. It could be argued that the flexibility of this approach is useful and leads teachers to responding to the needs of individuals, rather than being concerned with how much of their plan they should have covered at any point in time.

However, Alex's view is also common and many unplanned lessons lack focus and coherence and this can lead to the learners becoming irritated. Jenny's view that planning simply takes too long has probably been felt by most teachers at some point in time. Teachers new to the profession can often find planning particularly onerous, although most teachers get much quicker at planning lessons as they gain experience. Often the amount of planning required can seem to expand to fill the time available and this should be avoided. Teachers need to learn to discipline themselves so that planning does not take up too much of their time. Gary comments that he changes his plan frequently. This is not necessarily a bad thing as it may be as a result of responding to the needs of individuals in the class. However, changes should be made in a fairly principled way with the teacher trying to think of the pros and cons of the changes they make.

Lesson planning checklists

This is a guide only. It could be argued that some of the questions could be relevant to other types of lesson, but in each case the list should help to achieve reasonably effective planning.

Vocabulary and grammar	**Receptive skills**	**Productive skills**
How will the meaning of the new language be conveyed? Has the form been covered adequately? Has the meaning been covered adequately? Has the language been presented in a common context or contexts? Will learner understanding of the new language be checked? Are there sufficient and varied practice opportunities? Is there enough/too much new language? How will language errors be dealt with? Have interaction patterns been considered?	Is there a lead in to the topic? Are there clear tasks and will they be set before the learners see the text? Is there too much new vocabulary in the text? Will learners have the opportunity to discuss answers? Would using time limits for tasks be helpful? How will problems in understanding be dealt with? Have interaction patterns been considered?	Is there a lead in to the topic? Will the focus be on fluency, accuracy or both? How will language errors be dealt with? Have interaction patterns been considered? Will the teacher/activity dictate the form and content of what is produced, or will the learners be free to produce the language they want?

Planning a series of lessons

1 This is probably not a good idea. Too much of one type of lesson may lead to boredom on the part of the learners. Variety is generally necessary. Also a learner who is absent for a day will miss one component of the course entirely.

2 At first sight this may seem an attractive idea because it could be assumed that learners will be tired and this will be more relaxing. However, if these activities are included in the course it can be assumed that they are thought to have some learning value and care should be taken not to send a negative message to the learners that they are not really very important. Some learners react negatively to such activities because they do not equate them with 'real' learning and teachers should be prepared to point out the language practice they offer.

3 and **4** Although this may seem a sensible division in many ways and is a useful guiding principle, language cannot be divided up quite so neatly. Grammar lessons, for example, may well include speaking and listening practice, and when helping learners with speaking a teacher may need to supply a piece of grammar or vocabulary. In 90 minutes there is often time to have more than one focus.

5 This is definitely good advice. In a series of lessons there should be links so that language is recycled but also plenty of variety in terms of type of input.

Selecting material

Advantages	**Disdvantages**
Course books save the teacher's time. Course books provide a coherent course with a sense of progression. The book provides a record of the course for learners to use as reference. Course books recycle new language. Course books grade material appropriately.	Continual use of one book becomes dull. No course book can reflect accurately the needs of a particular group. Course books are often produced for a mass market and ignore local needs and cultures. Course books tend to adopt a conservative approach to language teaching and restrict experimentation.

CHAPTER 17

ESOL and other teaching contexts

Although we have said that learners have different needs, most of this book has presented English language teaching as a unitary whole. However, this is not strictly true, because within English language teaching there are branches and subdivisions. The terminology used to describe these, often represented by acronyms, is not always used consistently and can become confusing. The divisions come about when the needs of the learners and the context of the teaching situation vary to such a degree that teachers must adapt their approach. However, typically the similarities to the type of approach described in preceding chapters will be far greater than any differences. In this chapter we will look at some of the various contexts in which teachers may find themselves working. We will start with ESOL teaching.

Teaching ESOL

By definition (see below) ESOL teaching takes place in an English-speaking environment, and so teachers working in contexts other than this may not find this section relevant.

Terminology

The terminology used can be confusing and requires clarification. English language teaching (**ELT**) is a useful umbrella term as long as it is remembered that the learners are non-native speakers. A further widely used term to cover different types of English language teaching is English for speakers of other languages (**ESOL**). These broad terms can be subdivided and we will look at three main divisions.

The first is English as a foreign language (**EFL**). This term is usually used for learners who choose to study English, either in an English speaking country or in their native country. As far as figures are available, it seems that around half a million students each year visit the UK alone to learn English. As far as teaching children is concerned, EFL is used to refer to studying English as a school subject where the rest of the curriculum is delivered in a different language. For example, school children in France may learn English as a foreign language, just as school children in England may learn French.

English as a second language (**ESL**) is a term usually used to refer to migrants, or other minority groups, learning English in a host country. For example, many refugees and asylum seekers would fit into this category. The learners may speak their mother tongue at home and in some social groups, but need to be able to use English to have full access to the wider community. However, increasingly **ESOL** is also used to refer to this situation, and this can lead to confusion given the previous use of this term described above. A further distinction is made for this situation when the learners are under 16. In these cases the term English as an additional language (**EAL**) is used.

ESL is also used to refer to people studying in their own country, where English is not the mother tongue, but where English is widely used in some aspect of life. In Singapore for example, English is an official language although many of the population are not native speakers. In the US ESL is used as an umbrella term for English language teaching to non-native speakers.

For the purposes of the rest of the discussion we will use ELT as an umbrella term covering all varieties of English language teaching to non-native speakers, EFL in the sense outlined above, and ESOL (in the second of the senses described above) rather than ESL because the trend seems increasingly to be to adopt this acronym.

How are EFL learners different to ESOL learners?

Look at the statements below. Which ones do you think apply to adult EFL learners and which to ESOL learners, as described above?

- Learners pay their own tuition fees.
- The state provides tuition.
- Learners have a low level of general education.
- Learners have a high level of general education.
- Learners learn English to further career prospects, or for pleasure.
- Learners learn English to survive in an English speaking environment.
- Learners may have suffered trauma in their own country.
- Learners are free to return to their own country at any time.

When you are ready, check your answer on page 127.

The answer provided deliberately paints a rather stereotyped picture because these are the views which have traditionally prevailed. However, all learners are individuals and this generalised picture is therefore inevitably, in part at least, inaccurate.

This is particularly true in regard to educational background, where the traditional view of the ESOL learner is being challenged. Although many ESOL learners have had few learning opportunities, others have studied to a very high level in their own country and this highlights the need to avoid using material which could be seen as patronising. It is easy to confuse a low level of English with a low level of general education.

Traditionally ESOL learners have been seen as needing to learn 'survival English'. If, when they arrive in the host country, they speak no English then this would be the overwhelming need in the short term. However, this view needs to be adjusted in the medium and longer term because people who wish to live independently in a society need to be able to do more with language than simply survive. Therefore the traditional view that ESOL is concerned with low level tuition needs to be re-examined and provision made for allowing learners to continue learning in order to maximise their potential.

Some ESOL learners have suffered trauma in their own country. The teacher needs to be aware of this possibility and therefore such EFL activities as 'tell your partner about your family' have to be approached with extreme caution or disregarded completely. The teacher needs to select material that will be unlikely to cause upset or offence. However, occasionally learners may want to talk about a troubled past, and this calls on the teacher to take on a role of concerned and interested listener. Teachers need to be sensitive and caring while retaining some professional distance.

However, despite the differences that can be identified, it should be remembered that learners of ESOL and EFL have a lot in common. Both sets of learners may want to learn English for work or study. Moreover, both types of learner are likely to see English as a means of communication which gives them access to new opportunities. As such they have a common desire to learn English quickly so that they can move on and use English to help them achieve their other goals.

Preparing to teach an ESOL class

Most of the methodology previously described for EFL classes will be appropriate for the ESOL classroom. Learners certainly still want relevant, motivating lessons that they perceive as being useful. They will need to learn to speak, listen, read and write, and the development of these skills will require an awareness of vocabulary and grammar. Learners will need to be involved in the learning process and the teacher will need to be ready to correct errors and to supply necessary bits of language. However, there are also some additional considerations and we will now move on to look at these.

Look at the following questions and try to answer them.

1 Would you expect the range of learner levels to be greater in an ESOL class or an EFL class?

2 Would you expect it to be easier to find material for an ESOL class or an EFL class?

3 Who will use English more outside the classroom, an ESOL learner or an EFL learner?

1 There is no definitive answer to this question. For various reasons levels can be quite mixed in either type of class on occasions. However, in addition to the usual variety of levels to be expected in any class, ESOL teachers often find that they have to deal with quite varying degrees of literacy, which is less often the case in an EFL context (see Chapters 8 and 10). Some learners may not be literate in their own language(s) and this can lead to difficulties in placing the learners into classes at an appropriate level because their speaking and listening skills may be dramatically better than their reading and writing abilities. This range of levels sometimes means that teachers have to use 'differentiated' material within a class. This means that some learners may use one piece of material and other learners a different piece, or the same piece may be exploited in different ways. Clearly this requires very careful planning, with the needs and abilities of each individual in the class being fully considered. Where such a range of level exists, some institutions may try to provide a teaching assistant to help the qualified teacher.

ESOL learners within any one class may also have a wide variety of backgrounds, both educationally and culturally. This can lead to a wide range of expectations on the part of the learners both in terms of course content and methodology used. The teacher needs to take account of these expectations and where necessary explain the approach being used.

2 It is generally much easier to find material for EFL learners. EFL classes exist all over the world, providing a vast market for publishers, several of which produce course books and supplementary material at a range of levels. However, there is relatively little material published for ESOL learners because the potential market is that much smaller.

It could be argued that as ESOL learners are living in the UK on a permanent basis, they need to be exposed to relevant authentic material (that is material that was not originally designed for teaching purposes) earlier than EFL learners. For example, an ESOL learner who wants to register their child for a school will probably need to complete certain forms. A simplified form which may be found in an EFL course book to help develop writing skills may prove of limited value to such a learner. Exposure to authentic forms and guidance on how to fill them in is likely to be more beneficial.

In the UK the Adult ESOL Core Curriculum forms the basis of all ESOL teaching.

It was introduced in 2001 by the Department for Education and Skills in a bid to improve the 'quality and consistency' of ESOL teaching. It aims to provide a 'comprehensive framework to help identify and meet each individual's language learning needs'. The document runs to over 400 pages and can be a little daunting for new teachers, but as teachers become more familiar with its layout it can give some useful support. The main bulk of the work covers the curriculum requirements for learners at the levels of Entry 1, Entry 2, Entry 3, Level 1 and Level 2 (as specified in the National Qualifications Framework). Each level is then subdivided into the skill sections of speaking, listening, reading and writing.

One of the most useful features of the document is that sample activities are given for each point in the curriculum. Teachers do not have to use these activities but many of them will prove helpful. Most of them require some preparation (for example, although sample dialogues are included they have not been recorded) and teachers will also need to supplement the activities given.

There is a referencing system used throughout the curriculum so that schemes of work and individual lesson plans can indicate which sections of the curriculum have been covered. Teachers should identify the parts of the curriculum which will form the basis of the course, and then look at putting the sections into a logical sequence. The information and ideas for each section can then be used to help in writing a specific lesson plan. Teachers may find it useful to make notes on their plans after each lesson (regarding what worked well, what didn't work, what caused problems and so on) and then file the plans so that they can form the basis of future lessons if the course is repeated.

3 Again, there is no definitive answer to this question, particularly as the context for EFL learning can vary greatly. However, what can be said is that although ESOL learners are by definition resident in an English-speaking environment, they do not necessarily use English to a great extent outside the classroom. They may well live in family and social groups in which their mother tongue is used almost exclusively. This means that some ESOL learners tend to use English only when trying to engage the services of another. For example, when they go to the doctor. In such situations language exchanges are often organised on a question-answer basis, with the ESOL learner usually in the role of respondent. Teachers need to provide input on question forms so that learners are more fully empowered in such exchanges. Learners also need to become familiar with communicative exchanges which are not dominated by question-answer patterns, so that they can take part in them more effectively.

The methodology used for EFL and ESOL learners is not greatly different, but ESOL classes often present teachers with additional challenges and careful planning is essential, particularly for inexperienced teachers.

Teaching business English

Many people need to use English for business purposes and the methodology used to teach those people is broadly the same as that described in the preceding chapters. The learners will need to develop at least some of the four skills and also learn new vocabulary and grammar. The main differences will be in **what** vocabulary and grammar is taught, the contexts in which it is taught, and also which skills are developed.

Types of learner

It is important to distinguish between two types of business English learner. One already has experience of working and therefore often has a very clear idea of the ways in which additional language skills could help them in their working lives. For this type of learner it is very important that the teacher works closely with them either before the course begins, or at the start of the course, to find out exactly what their needs are. Lessons can then be designed to meet these needs. (For an example of a simple needs analysis form, see Appendix 4.) Of course, over time the needs of the learners may change and so teachers need to be prepared to check whether this is the case.

The second type of business English learner may have no work experience or not have a specific job in mind. They simply feel that having a good command of English, particularly in the context of work, will help them to get a good job in the future.

In both cases it is important for the teacher to remember that their job is not to teach business skills, but language skills in the context of business. Teachers do not need a detailed knowledge of business, although some knowledge is clearly an advantage. What is essential is that teachers are interested in the topics that are covered and can relate to their learners and learners' interests (as with any other teaching). They need enough subject knowledge to be able to ask intelligent questions of their learners and to be able to find suitable, motivating material.

Methodology

The methodology used with a business class will be little changed from that used with a standard EFL class. For example, a lesson on direction giving with a standard EFL class may include such expressions as 'go straight on', 'turn second left' and so on. With a business class this may become 'take the lift to the second floor, turn left, the office is at the end of the corridor', but the need to provide practice, to correct learners and to involve them remains the same for both groups.

To give another example, having discussed needs with the class the teacher may decide that describing processes is particularly important. The teacher then needs to think carefully about the language which would seem natural to achieve this and then focus on teaching it. In this example there are two obvious areas to be covered.

Processes can usually be broken down into stages and so the learners may benefit from learning set expressions that can be used for sequencing – 'first', 'next', 'the next stage', 'after that', 'later' and so on. The teacher may also decide that the passive voice should be taught in this context. So, the learners may need to be able to use language such as 'the chemicals *are mixed* in this machine…'.

Notice that the starting point for the lesson is not 'the passive voice' but a situation (describing processes) that the business English learner can easily relate to. The grammar input is then tailored to this specific need, with learners being able to see clearly the benefit of the lesson.

What vocabulary and grammar would you teach to a group of business English learners to describe company history?

When you are ready, check your answer on page 127.

Material

The material used for skills development with business English learners also needs to be carefully chosen. If learners are already working, then it can be a good idea to use the texts that they actually have to read or listen to in their jobs. If this is not possible, then try to choose texts which are as similar as possible and think of helping learners to develop strategies for coping with difficulty. If learners are not already in work, then the choice of texts should obviously still be related to business, and should not focus on one particular job but a range of jobs. In addition, business English students often have a greater need to develop writing skills than their general learner counterparts because they may need to write letters, faxes, emails, reports and so on. They may also need to give presentations, which require the ability to speak for longer uninterrupted periods than most learners need to.

There are many business English course books available on the market which can be very useful to a teacher. However, the teacher should be wary of automatically working through the book unless they are sure that it is meeting the needs of the learners. This is particularly true where the learners are themselves very aware of their needs, usually in cases where they are already working.

Teaching one-to-one

There are many reasons why learners may choose to have lessons on a one-to-one basis rather than as part of a group. The main benefit is that the course will be tailored to the exact needs of the learner. As a member of a group, there is always a need to compromise and accept that others may have different needs, different learning styles and preferences. However, in the context of one-to-one learning and teaching, there is no need to consider the preferences of others. This obviously highlights the necessity of the teacher investigating the exact needs and expectations of the learner. (For a simple needs analysis form, see Appendix 4.)

However, there are also some disadvantages of one-to-one lessons. For example, there is no opportunity to practise speaking in a bigger group, and there is no support and camaraderie that can come from being part of a group. These factors mean that the teacher needs to consider their role very carefully. For example, they must be prepared to be a participant in the lesson, as well as performing the other roles that a teacher has. This participation may be in the form of acting as a partner in pair work activities, for example.

In a one-to-one lesson the relationship between the teacher and the learner is likely to be more equal than in a group situation. The teacher needs to consider where s/he sits and the effect this will have on the lesson. By sitting next to the learner a collaborative feeling is created. Often teachers choose to sit at roughly 90 degrees to the learner because this still creates a collaborative feel but allows eye contact to be made more easily. The equality of the relationship between learner and teacher is emphasised in the one-to-one context and this places an additional need on the teacher to listen carefully to the learner and to respond appropriately.

It may be that in some one-to-one lessons there will be very limited traditional classroom resources because they may take place in someone's home or office. However, a piece of paper can easily be used for everything a board would traditionally be used for and when placed between the learner and teacher can be used collaboratively and also be taken away by the learner as a record of the lesson.

One-to-one teaching activities

Activity 1

The teacher asks the learner about what they liked doing as a child and how they spent their time. After a minute or two the teacher asks the learner if s/he would mind answering similar questions, but on tape. The teacher records the exchange, and asks additional, related questions so that the exchange lasts between 5 and 10 minutes. The teacher plays the tape back and praises good language use and highlights any mistakes. If necessary the exchange is re-recorded. The teacher tells the learner that they will record another similar exchange, but this time rather than just the teacher asking questions, the learner should also try to ask appropriate questions of the teacher, so that a more realistic and equal exchange is created. Again, the recording is analysed afterwards.

Notice that the lead in is not recorded, allowing the learner to perform without pressure, and the rehearsal helps the next phase. The recording makes it easy for the teacher to split their roles of participant and teacher. The material is also highly personalised. The learner has a chance to prepare for each stage. The lead in helps the first recording, and it is not until the learner has answered questions that they then take on the more demanding role of both answering and asking questions. Notice too that the teacher contributes in the final exchange by answering questions as well as asking them, making the status of the roles of the participants fairly equal.

Activity 2

The teacher tells the learner to imagine that they want to book a holiday by telephone. They work together to think of the information that may be required and rehearse the appropriate questions. The teacher then asks the learner to telephone him/her at home that evening and they role play the situation with the teacher supplying the information requested. In the next lesson, the teacher goes through the exchange with the learner, again highlighting what was good and also areas that require further work.

Notice how the role play is prepared for in the lesson, so that success is likely, rather than failure. Notice too how both these activities exploit the potential of the one-to-one situation. Neither of them would be possible with a big group of learners but are easy to carry out on a one-to-one basis.

Teaching young learners

When using the term 'teaching young learners' we need to be very clear on what is meant because there are clearly very big differences between teaching 4 to 6-year-olds and 14 to 16-year-olds. Again, however, there are similarities, perhaps the most important of which is that in both situations one of the main responsibilities of the teacher is to leave the learners with a positive feeling about learning, so that they are motivated and want to continue their studies.

Particularly at the younger end of the spectrum, learners generally do best by 'learning through doing'. This may take the form of singing songs in English, which often helps with different aspects of pronunciation, including stress and intonation. Playing games is also popular, as are activities such as drawing and colouring in a picture. For example, the teacher could teach a few items of clothes vocabulary, and then have the learners draw a picture of a person. The lesson is carried out in English as far as possible and learners pick up some language as they go along. The teacher supplies bits and pieces of language as they become necessary and circulates around the room asking questions such as 'What colour will you colour her shirt?'.

Teenagers often respond well to discussion activities and a similar approach can be used to that with adults, including the use of correction techniques. Finding material that interests a class can be difficult but sometimes learners can find material that they want to use and bring it into class.

Teachers often worry about discipline with younger learners (see Chapter 3), and management can sometimes be difficult. It is generally a good idea to stop activities a little earlier than would be the case with adults and to have plenty of changes of focus in the lesson so that the learners have a feeling of being busy and are then less likely to go 'off-task' and become disruptive.

Often with young learners there may be a syllabus that is set out by a government department or some other body, and this must be worked through, but this is not always the case. Where teachers have the chance to design the course, listening and speaking lessons are often popular, along with vocabulary, including set phrases that can quickly boost fluency and the ability to communicate.

Young learners' teaching activities

Activity 1 – very young learners
The teacher shows the class some pictures of animals (about eight) and tries to elicit what they are called. The class repeats the word after the teacher and then the teacher writes the word on the board. The teacher puts the pictures around the room and says one of the words. The class move and touch the appropriate picture. After a few goes, a learner takes over calling out the words. After a few more goes the teacher asks the class to sit down. The teacher distributes either a picture or a card with one of the words on it to each person in the class. The learners circulate and try to find their partner, so that words and pictures are matched. When they have managed to do this, they stick the word and the picture on the board together. The teacher gives each learner a piece of paper and asks each child to draw one of the animals and write the word underneath.

Notice that there are several parts to this activity, all dealing with the same language point. Also notice that the focus for the most part is on learners recognising, rather than producing, the language. Notice too that there is a lot of physical movement in the lesson.

Activity 2 – not so young learners
The class works together to make a video. The teacher introduces the idea of making up stories and leads the class to agree on a story line and the characters involved. The learners work in groups to produce a script for a sequence of the story, each group writing a different part of the story. When the story is complete, the class agrees on who should act which parts. The final version is videoed and then played back to the class.

This activity could be spread over several lessons, and can be very motivating. The language input is gradual, with the teacher offering support and help at each stage of the activity. Typically learners of this age respond well when there is a final product from the activity – in this case the video.

Whatever age of young learner you are teaching, it is important to make the class feel busy and purposeful. Learners need to feel engaged in and enthused by what they are doing and although a range of course books are available for learners of any age, it is likely that the teacher will need to supplement these to ensure that there is sufficient variety to retain the motivation of the learners.

Teaching exam classes

One reason for learners taking language courses is that they need to pass an exam. The exam may allow them to progress in their education or professionally, for example. There are several exam boards that provide EFL exams and many different exams and it is quite common for teachers to be expected to teach exam classes.
Before you read on, think for a few minutes about the following questions.

1. As a teacher what would you do before the course began?
2. Would you make any changes to the content of a standard course if you were teaching an exam class?
3. Would you expect the learners to behave any differently?

There is no big shift in teaching methodology when teaching exam classes. However, the design of the syllabus will be affected by what learners have to do in the exam. For example, if learners have to write a lot in the exam, then you would expect writing skills development to be an important feature of the course.

It is clearly very important that the teacher is familiar with the organisation and test types used in the exam. Exam boards are not secretive about this information. Their web sites will often provide very up to date details and can be found easily by putting the title of the exam into a search engine. They may also publish 'exam reports' which detail how candidates performed in recent exam sessions. This can be a useful guide for teachers and their students because they can see how the exam is marked and what examiners expect. ELT publishers provide a wealth of material that teachers can use to prepare students for the most common exams.

An appropriate balance between exam practice and language development can be difficult to achieve. Obviously students need to know what will happen in the test and to have practised the different test types used in any one exam (essay writing, multiple choice questions, oral interviews, and so on). On the other hand, exams are a measure of language ability and time needs to be devoted to simply trying to help the learners become better at English. The balance may shift over the course, so that the teacher starts with only small amounts of exam practice at the beginning of the preparation course and then gradually increases the exam focus.

The learners may well be a little different in exam classes. Usually they have been 'screened' to ensure that all of them have a realistic chance of passing the exam. This may involve sitting a short test in order to be accepted for the course. However, there are financial considerations that course providers may have to make, and language level may not be the sole criterion of being accepted onto a course. Once in the class, learners tend to be very motivated because they have a clear goal and will work very hard to achieve it. The teacher must be prepared to provide (and mark) quite a lot of homework, perhaps more than would be produced by other classes. This learner motivation needs to be fostered by the teacher. There are times when learners need a great deal of encouragement and positive feedback about their chances in the forthcoming exam, and yet there are other times when learners need to be told very clearly how much work they need to do and what they need to improve upon to have a good chance of passing. The teacher needs to consider which learners need to hear which message at which times.

Summary

- EFL and ESOL learners share much in common but there are also significant differences.
- Teachers of ESOL may need to deal with a wider variety of levels and will find appropriate published material harder to find.
- Teachers of business English and those dealing with learners on a one-to-one basis need to prioritise responding to learner needs.
- Teaching young learners is often most effective when a 'learning by doing' approach is adopted.
- Learners in exam classes need to develop both their overall language ability and become familiar with the demands of the exam.

CHAPTER

17 Commentary

Teaching ESOL

How are EFL learners different to ESOL learners?

This is a suggested answer but inevitably deals in part with generalisations and stereotypes.

EFL	ESOL
Learners pay their own tuition fees. Learners have a high level of general education. Learners learn English to further career prospects, or for pleasure. Learners are free to return to their own country at any time.	The state provides tuition. Learners have a low level of general education. Learners learn English to survive in an English speaking environment. Learners may have suffered trauma in their own country.

Teaching business English

A lesson on company history would involve the teaching and practising of the past tense. The teacher may also have to teach vocabulary such as: *to form, to found, to establish, to merge, a merger, to expand, to take over, a takeover* and so on.

CHAPTER 18

Professional development

Initial training

This book has aimed to help people who may never have taught English before to move towards becoming competent and professional teachers. There are many courses available, most notably those run by Cambridge ESOL and Trinity College, *London*, that are designed for people with no experience of ELT. Some of these courses are very good and most participants see genuine progress in a short space of time. However, it is very important that those following such courses remember the limitations of them as well as the strengths. For most people it takes time to become a confident teacher. The more hours you spend teaching the better you are likely to become at doing it and in many ways, when someone finishes their initial training and gets their first job, then their learning really begins. In this chapter we will look briefly at how teachers can continue to develop professionally after their initial training has been completed. We will also look at the career options that are available for teachers as they gain experience.

Continuing professional development

Teachers need to understand that after initial training there is still a lot to learn about their chosen profession. There are largely two types of development that teachers need to explore.

The first is to consider all the ways in which the teacher can learn and improve independently. The second is the way in which a teacher can learn from the experience of others. Teachers can help themselves by reading about teaching. There are numerous books, journals and web sites that will help with everything from theoretical issues and linguistics to providing ready prepared lessons. The internet has become a major source of material for teachers and much of it is available free of charge.

Another important way in which teachers can help themselves is to think carefully about what they do. People often say that making a mistake is a learning experience, but this is only so if it is recognised as a mistake and the reasons for it are carefully thought through. Teachers need to reflect on their practice, thinking about what worked well and what things didn't in any particular lesson. The more teachers can work out **why** things went well or badly, the better chance they have of adopting appropriate techniques in the future. For new teachers it can be useful to set aside a few minutes before planning a lesson to think about recent lessons. Learning to reflect on your practice is an essential part of developing as a teacher.

Another very useful way of developing as a teacher is to think of your past experiences as a language learner, or even to enrol on a language course. How did you feel?

Was it ever a stressful experience? Were you involved in planning the course by telling the teacher what your needs were? Did everyone in the class have the same needs? What did you enjoy doing in lessons? What things didn't you enjoy? By placing yourself in the position of a learner, you will get a better understanding of the range of emotions that learners in your classes may feel at any given time. You may also learn some good strategies for how to cope with different classroom situations.

As well as helping themselves, teachers can draw on the experience of others and colleagues are usually happy to help. There are three main ways in which the experience and knowledge of others can be tapped into. The first way is by observing a lesson of a more experienced colleague. Watching experienced teachers is an invaluable way of learning. It is a good idea to make a few notes about the things that you could incorporate into your own practice.

A second way of learning is to ask a more experienced colleague to watch a lesson you teach. It is a good idea to think before the lesson about what you would like to gain from the observation. For example, are there any weaknesses in your own practice that you are aware of but are struggling to make progress with? If so, your colleague, having seen you teach, may be able to help. It is quite usual for schools to arrange such observations, particularly of new teachers.

Another way of gaining from the experience of others is to attend workshops organised by the school. These are usually fairly informal and can be useful because they can target specific issues within the institution, as well as discussing broader topics. Sometimes workshops such as these go beyond just one school, and are organised to benefit all the teachers in a local area.

It is important that new teachers look for every opportunity to continue learning about their profession and developing as practitioners of it.

Where to find out more

There are many excellent publications about teaching and language. For English language teachers a grammar reference book is a very important tool. It is often a good idea to go into a bookshop and browse before buying until you find a book that suits you. However, the following are both excellent:

Michael Swan *Practical English Usage* (Oxford University Press)
Martin Parrott *Grammar for English Language Teachers* (Cambridge University Press)

There are a range of books available that have instant 'recipes' for lessons, often organised on a particular theme. They are usually part of a series of resource books for teachers offered by publishers. For example:

Mario Rinvolucri and Paul Davis – *Dictation* (Cambridge University Press)
Sheelagh Dellar – *Lessons from the Learner* (Longman)
Gillian Porter Ladousse – *Role Play* (Oxford University Press)

Such books usually come with an introductory essay on the organising theme of the book.

Some publishers also produce collections of lessons with material that is photocopiable. They are often more expensive because teachers can copy them freely for their classes.

In situations where it is not easy for a teacher to get to a bookshop, several offer excellent delivery services, such as The Keltic Bookshop (www.keltic.co.uk).

Teachers can also keep in touch with recent publications and developments by checking publishers' web sites:

http://www.oup.com/elt
http://publishing.cambridge.org/elt
http://www.longman.com
http://www.onestopenglish.com
http://www.deltapublishing.co.uk

Teachers could also subscribe to ELT magazines. Typically they balance theoretical and topical issues with some classroom ideas. Two such publications are:

English Teaching Professional (www.etprofessional.com)

EL Gazette (www.elgazette.com)

Teachers can also join professional organisations. Some schools and colleges have institutional membership of bodies such as IATEFL (International Association of Teachers of English as a Foreign Language), which individuals can also join. This organisation can be contacted at www.iatefl.org. Another option is the Association of Teachers of English to Speakers of Other Languages, based in the US, and contactable through its web site www.tesol.org.

Further courses

There are numerous courses that may be relevant for teachers to follow after their initial training. We will look briefly at three sorts.

In-service short courses

There are a number of schools and training centres that provide in-service courses for practising teachers. Often these will cover a particular area, such as 'Technology and language teaching', in great detail. These can be very useful to further develop areas of particular interest. All teachers are generally welcome regardless of the amount of experience they have or qualifications held. However, as such courses tend to be quite expensive, it is a good idea to check carefully that the course content matches your needs before enrolling.

Diploma courses

There are several Diploma courses available to teachers who wish to get an additional qualification. The British Council recognises the courses validated by Cambridge ESOL and Trinity College, *London*. Teachers may find other courses very useful, but it may be that employers are more sceptical about their value because of the lack of validation. Although validated courses may be slightly more expensive, they usually prove to be a better investment in the longer term.

Diploma courses can be followed on either a full time or part time basis. There is usually a written exam and also assessed teaching practice. Diploma courses can be quite demanding and anyone enrolling should ensure that they have the time available for the necessary study. Typically, teachers must have an initial qualification and a minimum of two years' experience before enrolling on a Diploma course, although some providers may have different requirements.

A teacher who holds the Diploma will usually find that they have better job opportunities, and it is a minimum qualification for many teacher training or management positions. Diploma courses remain fairly practical in nature, so teachers usually find them very beneficial and highly relevant to their working lives.

MA courses

Many universities offer MA courses in ELT and/or applied linguistics. The amount of teaching experience required to gain access varies from institution to institution and with the precise nature of the course. Most MA courses are less immediately practical than the material covered on a Diploma course. However, insights into second language acquisition theory, the nature of language and so on clearly inform nearly everything that teachers do. Although such insights tend to be a step removed from the level of 'what can I do with my class tomorrow?', an understanding of these issues is extremely useful in the longer term. MA courses are generally organised on a modular basis. This increases their flexibility and allows those on the course to follow their own interests more closely. Clearly, an MA will have more cache in academic terms than the other courses mentioned.

Whether employers prefer teachers to hold a Diploma or MA is difficult to answer because this varies from country to country and is also dependent on the sector in which the employer operates. Both types of course involve a large investment of time and effort on the part of the teacher and therefore it is worth considering both options carefully before making a choice. Anybody thinking of enrolling on either type of course should consider carefully what exactly they hope to achieve by doing it and how these aims will be best served.

Career prospects

Possible career paths and options will depend on many variables, most notably the country in which you are working and whether you are in the state or private sector. As one would expect, career advancement is often dependent not just on experience but also qualifications.

English language teachers are very lucky in that their skills are required in many countries around the world and this opens up the opportunity for travelling. Native speaker English teachers are particularly in demand in this regard, and moving on from place to place is not usually seen as a weakness when applying for jobs in the future. In fact, variety of experience – whether you have taught mono-lingual groups or multi-lingual groups, the levels at which you have taught, whether you have taught exam classes or business English and so on – is almost as important as the number of years' experience you have accrued.

After several years in the classroom some teachers decide they would like to cut down on the contact hours they have with students and become more involved in other areas. For most teachers in this situation there are two main options available to them. One is to move sideways into teacher education and training. Many of the skills required to be a successful language teacher can be transferred into helping others to become language teachers. Most people who move in this direction start by running small workshops for colleagues. This requires no extra formal training but allows you to get a little experience. If you wish to move on to courses which provide professional qualifications, such as Cambridge CELTA courses, or Trinity College, *London* Certificate in TESOL courses, extra training will almost certainly be required.

Some teachers prefer the option of moving into more managerial positions. Nearly all institutions will need some sort of management hierarchy in which teachers can play a part. This may involve the placement of new students, timetabling responsibilities, recruitment and so on. Either teacher training or management can be combined with some teaching duties, and it is beneficial that they are. It is hard to imagine that someone who is involved in teacher training could work for long without actually teaching learners themselves. Similarly, it can be difficult to manage other teachers without demonstrating that you are able to work effectively in the classroom yourself.

Before these options can be considered new teachers to the profession need to concentrate on gaining as much experience as they can in as many different teaching contexts as possible.

Job interviews

If you have never been interviewed for a teaching job before, here is a summary of some of the things you may be asked in an interview, or may like to ask your interviewer. Of course, interviews will vary enormously according to the type of institution you wish to work in and also the culture of the country in which you are being interviewed. Therefore these are only rough guidelines.

You may be asked about:	*You may like to ask about:*
• methodology – e.g. how would you teach 'can' for ability? • your strengths as a teacher • your development needs as a teacher • any teaching experience you have (including on a course) – levels, nationalities, etc. • material you are familiar with • in mono-lingual contexts, what you know about the first language and problems that learners are likely to have with English • what things make for successful lessons • how you would maintain learner motivation	• the profile of the learners you will be teaching – ages, levels of English, numbers in a class, mother tongue(s) • the support you will receive – observations, workshops, somebody to ask for guidance • the syllabus you will teach from • material used • equipment the school has (videos etc.) • working hours/ conditions • salary • holidays • health care (if outside your own country)

Summary

- Initial training courses are the start of a teacher's development, not the end.
- New teachers need to take every opportunity to continue their development.
- There is a variety of courses, some leading to further qualifications, available to practising teachers.
- Career opportunities often depend on additional qualifications, as well as experience.

APPENDIX 1 Basic grammar terminology

Generally teachers should try not to confuse learners by using lots of complex terminology. However, both teachers and learners need to know some basic terminology, not least because it will help learners to use reference works successfully. The following is a very brief guide to some of the terms which are commonly used to describe language.

Sentences and clauses

Sentences can be classified as **affirmative** (*Angela likes pizza*), **negative** (*Rachel doesn't like pizza*) or **interrogative** (*Does Becky like pizza?*). Some sentences have more than one **clause**. The sentence *Richard likes tennis but Debbie prefers golf* is made up of two clauses which are joined by the word 'but'. These clauses could be simple sentences – they do not need other words. However, some clauses cannot stand alone. The sentence *When I drive, I never drink alcohol* has two clauses. *I never drink alcohol* could stand alone grammatically as a sentence and is the **main clause**. *When I drive* cannot stand alone because the thought is not complete. It is a clause but cannot stand alone as a sentence. Clauses which are dependent on other words are called **subordinate clauses**.

This description is true of written language. Spoken language, on the other hand, is not always made up of 'complete' sentences, or even clauses. People sometimes use single words or phrases to communicate, and subordinate clauses may sometimes be used without another clause.

Subjects and objects

Tracy	sent	her boyfriend	a postcard
subject	**verb**	**indirect object**	**direct object**

Subjects typically come before the verb (see below for information on verbs) and indicate who or what does something (***I*** *met Angela at the supermarket*). **Objects** usually come after the verb and indicate who or what something was done to. (*He crashed* ***the car***). In some sentences there are two objects. For example: *I gave* ***my father a birthday present***. In this case, *my father* is the **indirect object**, answering the question 'to whom?', and *a birthday present* is the **direct object**.

Active voice and passive voice

English sentences can be constructed using either **active** or **passive** voice. The active form is much more common in most types of speaking and writing, and not all sentences can be 'transformed' into passive equivalents.

Becky invited me is an active sentence. However it can be made passive by using the verb *to be* and the past participle of the main verb: *I was invited by Becky*.

Notice that the subject of the passive verb corresponds to the object of the active verb. The factors which affect the choice of voice are very complex.

Nouns

Nouns are typically defined as being the names of things. For example, *perfume, television, computers, Charlie, cat* and *advice* are all nouns. Nouns can be either **countable** – meaning that they have a plural form, or **uncountable**, meaning that there is no plural form. For example, *cat* is a countable noun and is singular. *Cats* is the plural form. Nouns such as *money, advice* and *knowledge* are uncountable. They have no plural form. Some nouns can be used in either a countable, or uncountable way. For example:
There are three potatoes on the table. (Here 'potatoes' is a plural countable noun.)
He ate two fish fingers and a lot of potato for his tea.
(In this case 'potato' is an uncountable noun.)

Pronouns

Pronouns are words that can stand in place of nouns. Pronouns can be divided into groups:
Personal pronouns: *I, you, she,* etc.
Possessive pronouns: *mine, yours, hers,* etc.
Reflexive pronouns: *myself, herself, ourselves,* etc.
Relative pronouns: *who, which,* etc.

Adjectives

Adjectives are used to describe things. *Old, happy, sad* and *expensive* are examples of adjectives. Typically they can come before a noun (*an* ***old*** *car*) or after the verb *to be* (*She is* ***happy***). Notice that other verbs such as *looks, seems* and *sounds* could replace *is* in the above example, and adjectives can follow verbs such as these, too.

Verbs

Verbs typically describe actions, states or experiences. *Jump, run, live, dream* and *be* are all verbs. Verbs may be made up of more than one word: *Our cat was* ***put down*** *last week.* These combinations are sometimes called **multi-word verbs**.

Verbs where the past form and the past participle end in *-ed* are described as **regular** verbs. Those that do not follow this pattern are **irregular** verbs.

Verbs have several parts. The **infinitive**, or **base form** of the verb, the **past form** (formed by changing the base form of regular verbs to end in *-ed*) and the **past participle** (also formed by changing the base form of regular verbs to end in *-ed*). For example:

	An example of a regular verb	*An example of an irregular verb*
infinitive/base form	walk	begin
past form	walked	began
past participle	walked	begun
present participle	walking	beginning

The infinitive can be used with or without *to*. For example:
I desperately want ***to see*** *you* and *I can* ***swim***.

Verbs also have a **present participle** which is the *-ing* form of the verb:
Are you ***seeing*** *anyone at the moment?.*

As well as acting as main verbs, as described above, *do, be* and *have* are also **auxiliary verbs**. Auxiliary verbs have a purely grammatical function in a sentence. For example, they are used when changing affirmative sentences into negative or interrogative ones: *She* ***does*** *not eat meat.* or ***Have*** *you seen her before?* Auxiliary verbs are also used to create some verb forms: *I* ***am*** *going now.*

Modal auxiliary verbs (such as *can, may, might, will* and so on) can perform similar grammatical functions to the auxiliary verbs above, but also add a semantic meaning. For example, in the question *Can you swim?* 'can' is inverted with the subject to form the question (grammatical function) but adds the sense of 'have the ability to' – a semantic element.

Determiners

Determiners come before nouns, or adjectives and nouns. They include:
Articles: *a, an, the*
Demonstratives: *this, that, these, those*
Possessives: *my, your, his* etc.
Quantifiers: *lots of, some, any, many, much* etc.

Prepositions

Prepositions such as *of, at, to, on,* and *above* usually come before nouns or pronouns. For example:
Her keys were ***on*** *the floor.*

Sometimes prepositions have an important lexical function in a sentence. For example: *His flat is* ***above*** *the chip shop* (where 'above' tells us about location).

At other times the role of prepositions is primarily grammatical. For example: *It depends* ***on*** *your answer.*

Adverbs

Adverbs usually give additional information about verbs or adjectives.
I ***often*** *go to the cinema alone.*
She made her decision ***quickly*** *and later regretted it.*
She's ***very*** *good at explaining things.*
That's a ***really*** *nice colour.*

However, adverbs can add a more global comment to a part of a sentence, or a sentence, or a combination of sentences.
Ian: So how do I download stuff from the internet?
Kirsty: ***Basically*** *you just have to click on the menu bar…*

Conjunctions

Conjunctions join clauses into sentences. They often come in the middle of sentences:
The house has three bedrooms ***and*** *a nice garden.*
She works hard ***but*** *doesn't earn much money.*
She left her job ***because*** *she wanted a new challenge.*

Conjunctions can also come at the start of a sentence:
Although *he was tired, he kept trying to find a solution.*
While *he was thinking, the phone rang.*

APPENDIX 2 Verb forms and their common uses

Teachers need to highlight both the form and meaning of verb patterns. The meaning can only be fully determined when the context is clear, but below is a summary of some of the more common uses of verbs and some of the basic elements of formation. Notice the similarities between all the continuous forms (both in form and use) and also the perfect forms (both in form and use). For more detailed and complete information consult a good grammar book.

Note 1: The names of verb forms can be misleading. Present forms are not always used to talk about the present and past forms are not always used to talk about the past.
Note 2: There are many ways of analysing grammar. For example, the analysis of conditional forms here is very simplistic, but it follows common practice in most EFL course books.
Note 3: Many grammar books use the term 'progressive' in place of 'continuous'.

Verb form	Notes on form	Common uses
Present simple	Formed by the base form of the verb: *We **like** football.* Add 's' in the third person: *She **watches** television.* Use *do/does* in negatives and interrogatives: ***Do** you **like** football?* *She **doesn't work** here.*	To talk about habits and routines: *We usually get up late at the weekend.* To talk about states/things that are always true: *She lives in Santiago.* To talk about timetables and schedules: *My plane takes off at 9.00 tomorrow.*
Past simple	Change the base form to end in *-ed* (or equivalent for irregular verbs): *We **walked** all the way.* Use *did* in negatives and questions with the base form of the verb: *I **didn't go** out last night.* ***Did** he **tell** you anything?*	To talk about most completed actions in the past. The action may be short: *Charlie fell over* or long: *He grew up in Spain.*
Future forms	See also *present simple, present continuous, future perfect simple and continuous*	
	will + base form of the verb: *She **will** probably **lend** you the money.*	To make predictions about the future: *I think Italy will win the World Cup.* To give facts about the future: *She'll be 25 next birthday.* To express spontaneous decisions – things you decide at the time of speaking: *I'll phone you tomorrow.*
	be going to + infinitive: *I**'m going to look** for a new job.*	To talk about plans: *We're going to travel round the world next year.* To make predictions: *I think it's going to rain.*
Present continuous	Formed with *be* as auxiliary verb + *-ing* form (present participle) of the main verb: *She **is brushing** her hair.* *I**'m not talking** to you.* ***Are** you **leaving**?*	To talk about things happening at this time or around this time. These are temporary situations: *Rachel is living with me until she can find a place of her own.* To talk about plans and arrangements: *I'm meeting Laura at 8.00 tomorrow.* To describe changes: *The economy is getting stronger.*

Verb form	Notes on form	Common uses
Past continuous	Formed with *was/were* + *-ing* form (present participle) of the main verb: *I* ***was walking*** *home at that time.* *Where* ***were*** *you* ***going****?* *They* ***weren't playing*** *football when I saw them.*	To describe an action happening around a point in time: *I was playing football at 9.00.* To describe the 'background' to some other event: *I was playing football when I saw John.*
Future continuous	Formed with *will* + *be* + *-ing* (present participle): *She'****ll be sitting*** *on a beach this time next week.*	To say that something will be happening around a point of time in the future: *I'll be driving to work at 7.30.* To talk about planned future events: *The plane will be landing at 9.00.* To make predictions about things that are happening at the time of speaking: *What do you think Andrew is doing now?* *He'll be playing football, I expect.*
Present perfect simple	Formed with *have/has* + past participle: *I'****ve seen*** *her somewhere before.* *He* ***hasn't been*** *to China.* ***Have*** *you* ***worked*** *here long?*	To talk about an action at an indefinite point in the past: *Have you ever read War and Peace?* To talk about something started in the past and continuing into the present: *She's worked here for three years.* To talk about something which has recently been completed: *I've just done the washing up.*
Past perfect simple	Formed with *had* + past participle: *She* ***had left*** *the party before I arrived.*	To say which of two past actions or events happened first: *He had already hidden the diamonds when the police arrived.*
Future perfect simple	Formed with *will* + *have* + past participle: *He* ***will have finished*** *the work by tonight.*	To say how long something will have been in progress by a certain time in the future: *By next month I'll have lived in the same house for ten years.* To say that something will have finished before a particular point in the future: *She'll have finished the report by 2.00* Used with 'by now' to make predictions about things at the time of speaking: *Belinda has an exam today.* *I know, but she'll have finished by now.*
Present perfect continuous	Formed with *have/has* + *been* + *-ing* form of the main verb (present participle): ***Has*** *she* ***been working*** *here long?* *She* ***has been working*** *here for ages.*	To talk about something started in the past and continuing into the present: *You've been watching television for hours.* To talk about recently completed actions (particularly if there is still evidence of the action): *It's been raining – the grass is wet.*

Verb form	Notes on form	Common uses
Past perfect continuous	Formed with *had* + *been* + *-ing* form of the main verb (present participle): *He* ***had been walking*** *for hours when he saw the tiger.*	To say how long something had been in progress up to another past event: *They had been following him for days before the arrest was made.*
Future perfect continuous	Formed with *will* + *have* + *been* + *-ing* form of the main verb (present participle): *By midday she* ***will have been juggling*** *for eighteen hours.*	To say how long something will have been in progress up to a future time: *Come July 12, Dave will have been working here for ten years.*
'Zero' conditional	*If* clause includes a present form. Result clause includes a present form: ***If*** *you* ***leave*** *chocolate in the sun, it* ***melts****.*	To talk about things that the speaker feels are always true: *Workers are usually happy if you pay them lots of money.*
'First' conditional	*If* clause includes a present form. Result clause includes *will* + infinitive (or another future form). (*Will* could be replaced by another modal verb, such as *can, may,* or *might.*): ***If*** *I* ***see*** *her, I'****ll tell*** *her.* ***If*** *you'****ve*** *already* ***been*** *there, you* ***won't need*** *the map.* ***If*** *you* ***ask****, he* ***might help*** *you.*	To talk about things which are likely to happen: *If the weather is nice I might go to the beach tomorrow.* (There is a good chance the weather will be nice.)
'Second' conditional	*If* clause includes a verb in the past simple. Result clause includes *would* + infinitive. (*Would* could be replaced by another modal verb, such as *could* or *should.*): ***If*** *you* ***were*** *a millionaire, we* ***could buy*** *a new boat.*	To talk about things which are unlikely to happen or are imaginary: *If I won the lottery I would buy a big house.* *If I were Prime Minister I would ban smoking.* (Note: the past form does not indicate a reference to past time, but to the hypothetical nature of the statement.)
'Third' conditional	*If* clause includes a verb in the past perfect. Result clause includes *would* + *have* + past participle. (*Would* could be replaced by another modal verb such as *might, could* or *should.*): ***If*** *Sylvia* ***hadn't helped*** *me I* ***wouldn't have passed****.*	To speculate about how things in the past that cannot be changed, may have worked out differently in different circumstances: *If the Titanic hadn't hit the iceberg* (but it did hit an iceberg), *it wouldn't have sunk* (but it did sink).

APPENDIX 3 Phonemes of English

Consonants

/p/ **p**ot **p**a**p**er **p**en

/b/ **b**all ta**b**le **b**it

/t/ **t**alk **t**op boa**t**

/d/ **d**uck pu**dd**le pai**d**

/k/ **k**iss ca**k**e ba**ck**

/g/ **g**reen bi**g** **g**oal

/tʃ/ **ch**oose **ch**icken coa**ch**

/dʒ/ **j**ob **j**u**dg**e **j**oke

/f/ **f**rog **f**ish **f**eather

/v/ **v**an **v**alve **v**ain

/θ/ **th**in pa**th** **th**ink

/ð/ **th**at fea**th**er mo**th**er

/s/ **s**ome **s**un bu**s**

/z/ **z**oo bu**zz** wi**z**ard

/ʃ/ **sh**ip fi**sh** **sh**ut

/ʒ/ televi**s**ion plea**s**ure mea**s**ure

/h/ **h**ome **h**ouse **h**elp

/m/ **m**ade **m**other co**m**e

/n/ balloo**n** **n**o **kn**ow**n**

/ŋ/ si**ng** walki**ng**

/l/ **l**ots **l**ong be**ll**

/r/ **r**ight **r**ed **r**oad

/j/ **y**es **y**ellow **y**ou

/w/ **w**ant **w**ork **w**and

Vowels

/iː/ sh**ee**p gr**ee**n t**ea**m

/ɪ/ s**i**t sh**i**p k**i**tten

/i/ bus**y** happ**y**

/e/ **e**lephant r**e**d s**e**nd

/æ/ c**a**t **a**pple t**a**p

/ɑː/ c**ar** p**ar**k sh**ar**k

/ɒ/ b**o**ttom t**o**p p**o**t

/ɔː/ p**or**t s**or**t b**ough**t

/ʊ/ l**oo**k w**oo**d p**u**sh

/uː/ t**oo** f**oo**d ref**u**sal

/ʌ/ c**u**t sh**u**t **u**mbrella

/ɜː/ th**ir**st b**ur**st

/ə/ **a**go feath**er** **a**bout

/eɪ/ p**ay** gr**ea**t l**a**te

/aɪ/ t**ie** s**igh** **i**tem

/ɔɪ/ t**oy** b**oy**

/aʊ/ c**ow** gr**ow**l

/əʊ/ g**o** sh**ow** r**oa**d

/ɪə/ **ear** h**ere** cl**ear**

/eə/ ch**air** c**are**

/ʊə/ p**ure** act**ual**

APPENDIX 4 Materials for use with example lesson plans

Writing lesson

Dear Danijela

I've been living with my girlfriend for nearly three years now. I really love her and know she's right for me. But every time I mention getting married, she changes the subject, and last time she said she didn't think we were ready for that kind of commitment. Now I'm really worried in case she doesn't really want to be with me at all. What can I do?

Tom

Dear Danijela

I've been seeing a guy for about a year now, and everything is going really well. I'm madly in love with him and I think he feels the same about me. The problem is that he's a lot older than me – nearly fifteen years – and my friends all think I'm making a big mistake. I'm scared that I'm going to end up either losing the man I love, or my friends. What can I do?

Rebecca

Dear Danijela

My best friend has been going out with this guy for about six months now but I know it's not very serious and she's always stayed in touch with her ex-boyfriend. The thing is is that I've fallen in love with her current boyfriend. I can't stop thinking about him and I think he likes me, but I don't want to do anything that might upset my friend.

What can I do?

Claire

Dear ____________________

Your situation is probably more common than you think. There are plenty of good relationships where there is a bigger age difference than the one between you and your partner. What matters is how much you care for each other, not how old you are, and remember your friends should only be concerned with your happiness. If they are not, then they are not worth having as friends anyway. If this is right for you, and you obviously are sure that it is, then pursue the man you love with all your heart.

Danijela

Dear ____________________

This is a difficult situation and I think you should talk to your friend. If you explain how you feel about her boyfriend and if you are right that she really doesn't think this new relationship is worth committing to, then she may be more understanding than you think. She's sure to appreciate that you talked to her rather than went behind her back.

Danijela

Dear ____________________

You have to sit down and talk to your girlfriend. She may not want to get married, or she may not want to get married to you. There's a big difference. If it's the second of these it may cause a lot of pain, but it would be better to know now, than wait and wait for her if she doesn't feel the same way about you as you do about her. Remember, in a good relationship you can always be honest about how you feel about each other. On the other hand, she may just need a little more time.

Danijela

Reading lesson

BOURNEMOUTH
Advertiser
Your weekly newspaper

FUR ALARM

Polly the cat saves couple from blaze

Report by David Haith

A CAT which saved her owners from death in a fire last week is to be nominated for an RSPCA award.

Polly, a 13 year old tortoiseshell, could have escaped out of a cat flap as thick smoke engulfed the rooms of a house in Kimberley Road, Southbourne, as Jean and 64 year old John Pegg slept.

But Polly stayed on the couple's bed pawing and scratching 62 year old Jean's face.

The more Jean ordered her to stop, the more the puss persisted with her alarm tactics.

Finally Jean awoke and switched on the light to find the first floor back bedroom filled with black smoke.

She roused her husband who was able to escape down the stairs.

DENSE

From a bedside phone Jean called the fire brigade but found the smoke was too dense for her to leave the bedroom.

She said: "I survived by opening the window to breathe until the fire crew rescued me down a ladder."

The couple were both taken to hospital and treated for the effects of smoke.

The fire – started by an electrical fault in a freezer – gutted the kitchen and caused smoke damage to the rest of the house.

Polly was found outside by firemen, coughing and spluttering, but unharmed.

Said Jean: "There's no doubt that Polly saved our lives. She had been sleeping on our bed but in the early hours kept banging her paw very hard on my face. She kept doing it with her claws out so I'd wake up. She was also making this 'yak yak' sound – a noise she makes by banging her teeth together when she sees birds out of the window."

Jean added: "The firemen told us that the smoke was so thick we were within five minutes of dying. Polly is a heroine and I'm putting her name forward for an RSPCA bravery award."

Vocabulary lesson

Heart

What does this picture mean to you?

In your language, do you have any expressions that use the word 'heart'?

What do they mean?

Match the expressions in the box to the definitions below.

She broke his heart. ❤ We had to learn the dates by heart.
She's young at heart. ❤ He's a bit heartless. ❤ My heart sank when I saw the queue.
We had a heart to heart talk. ❤ He needs a heart transplant. ❤ I've had a change of heart.
Can you hear my heartbeat? ❤ He died of a heart attack.

a) a sudden and serious illness when the heart stops working

b) to make somebody very, very sad and depressed, particularly about love

c) to be very unkind and uncaring

d) to take the heart from one person and put it in another

e) the movement and noise made by the heart

f) a very personal conversation about feelings and emotions

g) to know something very well so that it can be repeated without thinking

h) to become suddenly disappointed

i) to change a decision or opinion

j) used to describe somebody who acts in a youthful, energetic way, even though they are not young

Try to answer the following questions as quickly as possible.

1 'To have a change of heart' – is this a medical expression?

2 Does 'heart to heart' describe talking or dancing?

3 If you learn something 'by heart', do you need to think before repeating it?

4 'To have a heart transplant' – is this a medical expression?

5 If someone is described as 'young at heart', is it a good thing?

6 If you 'break someone's heart', are they hurt physically or emotionally?

7 Can you think of an adjective to describe somebody hurt in this way?

8 If someone is described as 'heartless', is it a good or bad thing?

9 If your heart 'sinks', do you feel happy?

10 If you run for a long time, does your heartbeat get quicker or slower?

Questionnaire A

Complete the questions.

When you have finished, ask your partner the questions.
Ask 'follow-up' questions, too. Example:

A: Do you know anybody who is heartless?
B: My boss, definitely.
A: In what ways?
B: Well, when I…

1 Do you know anyone who is h________________s?

2 If you are watching television, does your h______t s____k when the telephone rings?

3 When you were at school, did you have to l______n anything by h_________t?

4 Have you ever felt h________________n?

5 Have you ever had a h_______t to h_______t t____k in English?

Questionnaire B

Complete the questions.

When you have finished, ask your partner the questions.
Ask 'follow-up' questions, too. Example:

A: Do you know anybody who is heartless?
B: My boss, definitely.
A: In what ways?
B: Well, when I…

1 How can people stay y_______g at h_______t?

2 What things can cause h_______t a_________s?

3 If you had a heart problem and the doctors said you could have a h_______t t_______________t from an animal, would you want it?

4 Have you ever felt strongly about something and then had a c_______e of h_______t?

5 Have you ever listened to your own, or anyone else's, h_______t?